Creating Change

**the arts as catalyst
for spiritual
transformation**

Keri K. Wehlander, EDITOR

Creating Change

the arts as catalyst for spiritual transformation

CopperHouse

Editors: Keri K. Wehlander & Ingrid Turnbull
Cover and interior design: Verena Velten and Margaret Kyle
Prepress Production: Chaunda Daigneault
Proofreader: Dianne Greenslade
Cover art: "Outside the Lines" © 2007, Margaret Kyle,
Okanagan Centre, BC, margaret@woodlake.com

FSC
Mixed Sources
Cert no. SW-COC-1271
www.fsc.org
© 1996 Forest Stewardship Council

CopperHouse is an imprint of Wood Lake Publishing, Inc. Wood Lake Publishing acknowledges
the financial support of the Government of Canada, through the Book Publishing Industry
Development Program (BPIDP) for its publishing activities. Wood Lake Publishing also
acknowledges the financial support of the Province of British Columbia through the Book
Publishing Tax Credit.

SILVER
BIBLIOGRAPHIC DATA 2008-09

At Wood Lake Publishing, we practise what we publish, being guided by a concern for fairness,
justice, and equal opportunity in all of our relationships with employees and customers. Wood
Lake Publishing is an employee-owned company, committed to caring for the environment and
all creation. Wood Lake Publishing recycles, reuses, and encourages readers to do the same.
Resources are printed on 100% post-consumer recycled paper and more environmentally friendly
groundwood papers (newsprint), whenever possible. A percentage of all profit is donated to
charitable organizations.

Library and Archives Canada Cataloguing in Publication

Creating change : the arts as catalyst for spiritual transformation /
Keri K. Wehlander, editor.
Includes bibliographical references.
ISBN 978-1-55145-568-6
1. Christianity and art. I. Wehlander, Keri, 1956-
BR115.A8C74 2008   704.9'482   C2008-904147-X

Published by CopperHouse
An imprint of Wood Lake
Publishing Inc.
9590 Jim Bailey Road, Kelowna,
BC, Canada, V4V 1R2
www.woodlakebooks.com
250.766.2778

Printing 10 9 8 7 6 5 4 3 2 1
Printed in Canada by
Friesens

ENVIRONMENTAL BENEFITS STATEMENT

Wood Lake Books saved the following resources by
printing the pages of this book on chlorine free paper
made with 100% post-consumer waste.

TREES	WATER	ENERGY	SOLID WASTE	GREENHOUSE GASES
14 FULLY GROWN	5,285 GALLONS	10 MILLION BTUs	679 POUNDS	1,273 POUNDS

 Calculations based on research by Environmental Defense and the Paper Task Force.
Manufactured at Friesens Corporation

Table of Contents

PART 5 – Transforming How We Learn

PART 6 – Transforming Churches

Introduction

April 12, 1888
My dear old Bernard,
Thanks for your kind letter and the sketch of your decoration included
with it, which I find really amusing. I sometimes regret that I can't decide to
work more at home and from the imagination. Certainly – imagination is a
capacity that must be developed, and only that enables us to create a more
exalting and consoling nature than what just a glance at reality (which we
perceive changing, passing quickly like lightning) allows us to perceive.

A starry sky – for example, well – it's a thing that I should like to try to do...
~ Vincent van Gogh

When I read these last few words from van Gogh for the first time, my eyes filled with tears. Written the year before he painted *The Starry Night*, they reveal a rich insight into the artistic process.

So often, it begins as a hunch, an intuition, a glimmer. You are riding the bus, and an image rises in your mind. You are folding the laundry, and a line of poetry begins to recite itself. You are walking out the door, and a melody begins to sound from someplace deep inside.

When we listen carefully to these inklings, we begin to shape something we haven't seen or heard before. Delving into the creative process, we gain insights from "aha!" moments, as well as encounters with dead ends. Both contribute to what is eventually created, and, ultimately, this process will shape us in unexpected ways. We can be certain that we will be transformed by what we create – and in turn, this finished creation may become a source of transformation for others.

The choice to create is a choice to risk. The capacity to take risks is what allows artists to tap into this transformative power. Artists recognize that there are no guarantees as to where that glimmer will lead – aside from the element of change.

Because I am a person rooted in the Christian tradition, I draw deep connections between the artistic process and the path of faith. I suspect that the Spirit is alive and well in many of those moments where a "nudge" comes from out of the blue. In light of story after story in the scriptures, it seems faith itself is full of risks. I also believe that the mere experience of transformation – be it big or small – is a reminder that hope is worth holding on to, because change is still possible.

I once had a conversation with Derek Evans, who has served as Deputy Secretary General for Amnesty International. Knowing that he possessed a wide international perspective, I asked him, "Where do you draw hope from?" He paused for a moment, and then began describing how he drew inspiration from the many groups of people who were working for positive change from within their own communities. He said that signs of hope were much more evident here than in the large institutional organizations within our societies.

As soon as I heard him speak these words, two thoughts came to mind. First, I had the image of a typical corporate newspaper, with headlines broadcasting the comings and goings of those with institutional importance. Next came images of all the people I knew in my life who were working for positive change in some way. It was like reading two completely different sets of headlines. And in spite of the fact that I had not worked at the kind of international level he had, I knew that I had experienced the same thing. Creative responses to problems are more likely to arise from smaller groups of people who are not bound by layers of formal structures.

A community central to the alternative set of headlines I carry within me is made up of artists I have come to know, either through their work or in person. I have relied on their songs, their images, their words, their dances – their sheer imaginations! – to breathe new life into the way I think and feel about my life and this world.

Frederick Buechner puts it this way:

The most basic lesson that all art teaches us is to stop, look, and listen to life on this planet, including our own lives, as a vastly richer, deeper, more mysterious business than most of the time it ever occurs to us to suspect as we bumble along from day to day on automatic pilot. In a world that for the most part steers clear of the whole idea of holiness, art is one of the few places left where we can speak to each other of holy things.[1]

Artists speak a language of holiness that I need to hear. And when this speaking of holy things through the arts meets a context of faith, remarkable possibilities open up. Spirits are nourished, new insights are embodied, communities are widened, our faith is deepened, and we are moved by glimpses of divine mystery.

This is what *Creating Change* is about: stories of individuals and communities who have been transformed in some way by the interplay between faith and the arts. If you could travel from community to community and ask people how their faith has been touched by the arts, these stories are some of what you would hear.

I believe that artists catch glimmers of what is just around the bend. I see artists working within church contexts who are re-imagining the music, images, stories, and language that are used within the tradition – all the while giving us new "signposts" for the journey ahead.

In her insightful book *Christianity for the Rest of Us*, Diana Butler Bass uses the term "signpost" for practices that were identified as common to vital and flourishing mainline congregations. One of the ten signposts that she names in her book is what she terms "beauty," or artistic expression, in the church. The chapter dealing with this is reprinted following this introduction, and I encourage you to read it before you turn to any of the other sections of the book.

If you are an artist, or you draw upon the arts as a source of inspiration, I hope that this book will be an encouragement to you. If you are hoping for insights or ideas around how to do this yourself, I hope that these stories will inspire and challenge you. If you are simply curious about what happens when art and faith meet each other, I know that you will find a story here that stays with you.

Whoever you may be, I hope that you hear my own gratitude for the rich gifts that artists have brought to my faith journey sounding from these pages. This book is a way of saying "thank you" to them for all those holy conversations.

– Keri K. Wehlander

---

[1] FREDERICK BUECHNER, *WHISTLING IN THE DARK: AN ABC THEOLOGIZED* (HARPER & ROW, 1988) P. 15

Beauty
Touching the Divine

Diana Butler Bass

My first visit to Redeemer in New Haven was on a very cold day. The chill wind cut through my down coat. The snow was deep, and topped by a thick crust of ice. The starkness of New England's winter impressed me anew. The same quality that haunts the season also marks New England Congregationalism, the region's native Protestantism, that unyielding Puritanism of early America. Especially in deep winter, the white clapboard Congregational churches add to the season's sense of spiritual void, the bleak beauty of a world frozen, as if perpetually awaiting the arrival of spring.

Unlike many of its sister Congregationalist churches, Redeemer is not white against the snow. It is brick. Although the color appears warmer than the traditional white, its architecture still exudes a familiar sense of Puritan austerity. I make my way up the stairs – careful to avoid any ice patches – and enter. The outside may be reddish-orange, but here, in the vestibule, everything is white. Through the doors, I see the large sanctuary, also white. Its plain interior replicates the older world of colonial New England. Clear glass windows, tall white columns, simple wooden pews, and a massive pulpit blend harmoniously. A large cross hangs in front of a curtain in the chancel. This is religion unadorned, just like Puritanism of the past. The architecture exists to frame the sermon, not distract from hearing the word of God. Only the light fixtures provide decoration – brass atomic-age chandeliers looking a little like UFOs hang above the pews. I try not to judge what this may mean to others, but it is not really my taste.

People enter quietly and take their places in the pews. The congregation is not big. I cannot imagine that a frigid January Sunday would draw a large crowd. From my seat, I count about one hundred resilient churchgoers. The organist plays Bach. From the rear of the sanctuary, the choir prepares the congregation for worship with a short piece called "Gathered Here." They sound professional, although I later learn that they are not. As they process to the front of the church, the congregation stands to sing. The hymn is "Joyful, Joyful, We Adore Thee," set to the tune of Beethoven's "Hymn to Joy."

Joyful, joyful, we adore thee, God of glory, Lord of love;
Hearts unfold like flowers before thee, praising thee, their sun above.
Melt the clouds of sin and sadness; drive the dark of doubt away;
Giver of immortal gladness, fill us with the light of day.

All thy works with joy surround thee, earth and heaven reflect thy rays,
Stars and angels sing around thee, center of unbroken praise.
Field and forest, vale and mountain, blooming meadow, flashing sea,
Chanting bird and flowing fountain, call us to rejoice in thee.

The sanctuary, so tranquil just a moment ago, explodes with music. Suddenly, the wintry space thaws into images of spring. The sparse congregation, its voices filling the space with song, seems at least twice its size. There will be many good words in the service – prayers, announcements, testimonies, and a sermon – but the words are interlaced with astonishing music. A piece called "Meditation" draws the congregation to quiet contemplation after the confession and pardon; a traditional hymn, "Fairest Lord Jesus," acts as a sung prayer; a Handel anthem offers praise to God; and, finally, an exquisite Telemann piece concludes the service. Played by a student who grew up in the church, the medieval music creates a sense of timelessness, as if the congregation is suspended in God. By the time the music ends, I am surprised to find myself gently crying.

In describing Redeemer to me, the Reverend Lillian Daniel said, "We are a church that cares about liturgy and music." That did not particularly surprise me. After all, the church sits right downhill from the Yale Institute for Sacred Music. Sitting and singing with them, however, I realized that more is involved than just caring *about* music. As the choir sang, many listened with closed eyes, seeming to experience an almost mystical sense of God's transcendence. And I was not crying alone; the medieval recorder brought a few other people to tears. These people *live* music.

Redeemer congregants are skilled at testifying. Yet, they struggle to explain what happens to them in music. Although it is hard to imagine in this brainy-Yale group, perhaps it is beyond their vocabulary. One woman fumbles a bit as she says, "It's not about performance; it's about drawing people to another place." Daniel, a member of the choir, says, "I came as a singer and then gradually came into the life of the church. That was a transformation as well, because the music was important to me but it began to take on another dimension." Natalie, an active member of the church, confesses that she "wouldn't be here if it weren't for the music."

Congregants ably connect the music to the biblical story, extolling, as one woman says, the way "the music fits the scripture." She continues, "It's not just the choir, but the music that we are singing as a congregation." Madeline, who has served as the church's moderator, says quite simply, "I love listening to it, I love rehearsing it, and I love singing it."

Many churches have excellent music, with concert-hall quality organists and choirs. Sometimes, though, fabulous church music can devolve into performance, with the congregation reduced to an audience and all the "action" happening with the musicians. In these cases, music becomes, to use an old phrase, the tail that wags the dog, undermining other church ministries. In contrast, at Redeemer, music, liturgy, and word were completely one, as were the choir, minister, and congregation. Indeed, the congregation appeared to be inside the music, not just watching a performance. It was a kind of grace-filled dance. And it was doing something spiritual to them. Together, they enacted the music, transforming their plain room with auditory beauty. In every sense, music at Redeemer is, as Kurt Mounsma told me, a *practice* – they work on making beautiful sound in community.

People attribute the power of the practice to the leadership of Marguerite "Maggi" Brooks, the music director whom one member called Redeemer's "soul." Maggi has been at Redeemer for twenty years, long before Lillian arrived. Under some circumstances, this might prove awkward for a new minister. However, the two women, who share a similar sense of liturgy and music, developed a genuine liturgical partnership. And, says Lillian appreciatively, "she's a fantastic musician." Maggi is indeed that – as well as professional and dignified. She also understands church music and the purpose of a worshiping community. Church is not just about the sermon or the music (or, as at some churches, the two competing). Rather "it's a total focus of the service which, if you do it right, the whole thing begins here," she says pointing at her heart, "and takes you out there." Like a conductor, she moves her arm gracefully heavenward. How do she and Lillian make that happen? "The Spirit drives us," she says gently.

Maggi grew up an Episcopalian and attended a church school where music was an important part of worship. Like other members of Redeemer, she easily relates her own spiritual journey and connects what happens in church to her gifts and passions. She has no formal theological training and, as she says, laughing a bit, "I spent a long time *not* in church." She mostly attended church to sing. Music shaped her. In recent years, she has studied the Bible and theology in more depth, but she insists that choral singing and studying at the Yale Institute helped her find God. She has wide experience of congregational music, and talks of experiencing God through the songs at a Jewish seder, in improvisational jazz, and in the music of a gospel choir. She speaks easily of "the beauty of simple songs"' and says, "I hear [God] with a different sort of ear."

Maggi's ability to listen led her to realize that not everyone hears God in the same way – that variety reflects the diversity of God and God's people. Although the overall style at Redeemer is classical, she draws from European, African, African-American, Native American, and other ethnic traditions. "I think to only do one kind of music is treating the congregation as a one-dimensional entity," she insists. "There is more to musical style than one style, regardless of what that is." She aims to touch the heart of every person in the congregation: "I try to aim for hymns that, at some point during the year, people will say, 'Wow, that's really the hymn for me!!'" Her emphasis is on paying attention to God's spirit, on maintaining excellence while being flexible and open. "Our music is not always musically of a piece," she confesses. "It would casually look pretty random to a musician." She smiles as she says, "Sometimes it really works."

It worked on Sunday in January. As I remember that day, I think of theologian Don Salier's words, "Whatever people can say with passion and in heightened speech they will end up singing in some form." Redeemer's people can certainly talk about faith, and in their practices of justice, they deeply live faith. No wonder they can sing! "When life is deeply felt," Saliers continues, "music gives shape and voice to the very pattern of our experienced world, through pitch, rhythm, and intensity, through lyrics and harmony. So, the act of singing together of life lived and felt binds heart and mind with ordered sound."[1] When connected to experience, pitch, rhythm, intensity, lyrics, and harmony create beauty. Redeemer's music painted that plain sanctuary with verbal image and vibrant color. The beauty of sound transformed the church into sacred space, as spiritually moving as any great medieval cathedral. We moved beyond austerity to the virility of God. The people at Redeemer may be the heirs of New England Puritanism, but they know the power of beauty.

A few years ago, I led a two-day workshop at an elite mainline seminary, renowned for its intellectual prowess, and stayed at the seminary's guest house. When I checked into my two-room suite, I could hardly believe my eyes. Everything was beige – walls, carpet, upholstery, bedspread, and towels. The chairs, pillows, and bed were hard. There was no television, radio, or CD player. No icons, crosses, not even a cheesy Bible-verse poster. Absolutely nothing in the room was warm, comfortable, or visually pleasing. The suite was plainer than any Roman Catholic monastery in which I had ever stayed, and its complete emotional and spiritual emptiness was appalling. God seemed utterly absent. Just one piece of art hung over the sofa: a large photograph of snow – with six shoots of wheat standing heroically amid the frozen tundra. I wondered if that was their vision of church – or, even worse, the Christian faith! If so, I thought ruefully, it would certainly explain their denomination's decline.

People expect Protestantism to be intelligent, but few expect it to be beautiful. Despite the fact that I was taken aback by the cold guest house room, perhaps others would expect such bleakness. After all, beauty is not the point. That is, after all, why people call us the frozen chosen.

For two centuries, American Protestantism has struggled between the poles of rationalism and mysticism – with rationalism most often winning. For most of the twentieth century, mainline religion has been associated with the life of the mind: learned theologians and Ivy League-educated clergy. Beauty has not been its strong suit. But that has not always been the case. In the late nineteenth century, against America's expanding industrial and technical culture, Protestantism exploded into a frenzy of romantic arts, music, and architecture. Mainline Protestants were taken by the mysteries of beauty, building vast neo-Gothic churches filled with jewel-like stained glass and intricate sculpture and carvings. The Protestant imagination went through a renaissance of poetry, painting, and the visual arts. Protestant theology emphasized emotions and ethics, moving towards ideals of beauty and mystery. These mainline ancestors were fascinated by history – especially that of medieval Europe and ancient Egypt – and by tradition. Across the country, congregations replaced or renovated their buildings, erasing all traces of early American rationalism in favor of the new emphasis on beauty.

In the early twentieth century, however, the trend reversed. Protestants began attributing all this exuberance to Victorian sensibilities, regarded as tasteless by the new generation of Christians. Protestantism defaulted to its historic rationalism. And any emphasis on beauty as a way to God was muted in favor of cool intellectualism. The beige utilitarianism of the seminary guest room only mirrored the aesthetic sensibilities of most midcentury Protestant modernism. But, on my journey, I had discovered that the tide was turning again. In the vital congregations I visited, rationalism was giving way to new expressions of beauty and finding God beyond words.

"I've only just recently come to the conclusion that I'm an artist and I can actually say that, and that's weird to me," said Alice Connor with a laugh. "Like many artists, I don't want to call myself an artist. But I do see, I understand things visually." She may feel awkward about the name, but she looks like an artist. Alice is a recent seminary graduate, still in her twenties, with closely shaved red hair, dangling earrings, numerous piercings, and a visible tattoo. She is ironic, mildly sardonic, edgy, and hip; her husband is a writer.

She may well be an artist, but she is also the Reverend Alice Connor, an Episcopal priest. At Redeemer in Cincinnati, she serves as assisting clergy working with youth. "I'm a big fan of reasoning things out and trying to make connections," she says. "I'm right there, but we need more than that. For me, aesthetics are part of it and I can't live without it. To me, God is beauty, and God created us in God's image. I can't live without that beauty." I wondered what she would have thought of the seminary guest room's beige God.

I heard remarks like Alice's all along my pilgrimage. In every congregation I visited, there was a growing emphasis on beauty, on knowing God through art, music, and drama, on engaging more than just the mind. Alice considers herself an intellectual and enjoys philosophical speculation – especially arguing about theology and politics. She says that although many people think that "we can reason God out in our minds and that's enough," she believes there are some things "our big brains" cannot figure out. Instead, she insists, "words and pictures speak to me." She says that she finds paradox "beautiful," and that certain ideas about God speak to her only "on a physical level."

For Alice, one such idea is the Christian doctrine of the Trinity, that God is both One and Three at the same time. (Thomas Jefferson once referred to this as the "incomprehensible arithmetic of the Trinity.") "I was opposed to the doctrine of the Trinity for so long." She laughs. "It is still difficult," she confesses rather boldly, "but the best argument I've heard is that rather than One of two – or One of eighteen – or 653 in One – we have One in Three because it's so elegant." She laughs again. "After this huge argument in seminary and after reading the church fathers and mothers and reading all this theology and not getting it – just arguing and being angry – my professor said that. It is elegant. And I said, 'Ah! I get it. That makes sense.'"

For Alice, beauty is the doorway to understanding. And she is not alone; the impulse toward melding beauty and speculation is strong among younger Americans. Indeed they may well be creating a new way of thinking theologically – a way that springs from the experiencing of beauty. Alice's testimony reminded me of a similar story that I heard from the writer Phyllis Tickle.

Phyllis was speaking at a large southern cathedral. About five hundred people, mostly baby boomers and older, attended her lecture. During the question-and-answer period, someone asked what she thought about the Virgin Birth. As such questions invariably do, this one devolved into a discussion of whether the Virgin Birth was a matter of scientific and historic fact.

As the discussion got more heated, Phyllis noticed that a young man, about seventeen years old, who was helping set up refreshments in the back of the room, had stopped his work to listen. She could see him on the steps leading to the balcony, listening intently to the exchange. When she closed her lecture, he came up to talk with her privately. "Ma'am," he said politely, "there's something I don't understand."

In her enormously generous way, Phyllis asked him, "What don't you understand?" She was ready to expound upon the complexities of the Virgin Birth with the young man.

His response, however, forestalled her explanation. "I don't understand why everyone is so upset about this," he said. "I believe in the Virgin Birth. *It is so beautiful that it has just got to be true – whether it happened or not.*"

Later, Phyllis told me that she felt as if the universe had shifted. "It is a whole new world," she said to me. "He had moved beyond mere facts to understanding based on apprehending beauty. I felt like I was standing on holy ground."[2]

Some people refer to this turn of intellectual events as "postmodern," a shift away from Enlightenment reason toward more experiential forms of knowing. I have heard some church leaders decry this development as somehow threatening to faith. However, both Alice's and the young man's remarks are rooted – perhaps unawares – in an ancient thread of American Christianity. At the height of theological rationalism in the eighteenth century, the much-misunderstood Puritan theologian Jonathan Edwards suggested that the apprehension of beauty, what he called "the divine and supernatural light," was the pathway to true Christianity, and the only possible antidote to intellectual and spiritual aridness. Although early American theologians revered Edwards, few substantially developed this aspect of his thought. Except for its flirtation with romanticism in the nineteenth century, much of American Protestantism walked straight into the trap laid by Enlightenment reason – a universe with no God, devoid of the Spirit's supernatural touch. By the time I was growing up, mainline Protestantism amounted to little more than secular church.

Perhaps unexpectedly in this highly technological age, young adults may well have found their way back to an untapped stream of American theological mysticism. Postmodern and ancient at the same time, new and old, innovative and traditional. One of Alice Connor's paradoxes. Truth is moving beyond the categories of Reason, beyond provable facts to a different realm. Christianity is changing – from being the Truth of rational speculation to being an exploration of the exquisite truthfulness of beauty.

All this reminds me that God is, indeed, elegant. And, as scientists, physicists, and philosophers are now teaching, God's universe is equally elegant – a quality that Christians believe creatively bespeaks God's being. Moreover, there is a remarkable elegance to those mysterious Christian things like the Trinity, the Virgin Birth, and resurrection. They may or may not have happened, but they are certainly beautiful.

In Asheville, North Carolina, Molly Easton testified about coming to deeper faith. In the 1980s, when she was still in her thirties, her husband died.

In the midst of personal crisis, she sought out the comfort of church. Through a friend, she found her way to All Souls Episcopal Cathedral, a small church that sits on the edge of the old Biltmore estate, right in the center of quaint Biltmore Village. Built in 1896 by the noted architect Richard Morris Hunt, the building is considered one of the prettiest churches in the country. Shaped in the form of a Greek cross, the interior is literally a masterwork of stained glass, painting, and carving – all carefully designed to convey the romantic vision of the late nineteenth century, with its passion for beauty and its recognition of the medieval ideal of apprehending God through the heart.

Molly confesses that she became "hooked on all things All Souls, starting with the people, then the liturgy, the music, the furnishings, and the architecture." She said:

> *It makes little difference whether the church is filled to overflowing on Christmas Eve or if I am the only one in the building, I find a sense of communication with the Holy One; however, when the choir is playing and singing and the sun is shining through one of the stained glass windows, that conversation is raised to a higher level. I have been close to tears at the visual impact of the colors rippling through a newly commissioned banner or the flood of light from the west sun turning Charity's halo to gold.*

In sum, Molly says, "I find the whole aesthetically pleasing and I find peace in a not so peaceful world." She believes that many of her fellow parishioners share her experience: "Art and architecture, you might say, helped to lead us to All Souls and opened the doors to a deeper spiritual life."

All Souls is known for hosting notable arts events and for its creative use of the arts in congregational worship. Todd Donatelli, the priest who currently serves the cathedral, believes that the arts create an environment that is "safe enough" to allow people to listen to God. Quoting a noted Quaker theologian, Todd says, "I think that is what Parker Palmer means when he speaks of 'hearing things slant.'" We can "hear," Todd insists, because the arts "speak afresh" Christianity's ancient texts in physical, embodied ways. In this way "the arts can also speak and connect us to the divine when we are too weary or simply have no words to offer," says Todd. People seem to natively understand this approach to faith. "I am continually amazed," says church member Tom Allen, "at the ability of hymn texts and anthem texts to move me to tears, slipping around every defense I possess, and rocket right to my heart." Or as Douglas Hart, another member of the parish, says more simply, "I think art is a refined form of prayer."[3]

At All Souls, the arts frame the spiritual life. As at Redeemer, though, they are not just performance or show. The arts link to other Christian practices, things like prayer and hospitality. Perhaps most surprising, however, is the relationship between the arts and social justice. All Souls was instrumental in founding the Church of the Advocate, a nongeographical "worshiping community" for homeless persons. Advocate is not a conventional church in any sense of the word, partly because it meets in shelters across Asheville. One of the ways in which Advocate works to support its members – and local homeless ministries – is through artwork and music. All Souls support the homeless congregation by showing and selling its art, including a music CD produced by Advocate members. Thus, at All Souls, beauty is not just a practice of personal spirituality or tasteful worship. Rather, the arts connect All Souls' people to both God and their neighbors – providing a way, to use Todd Donatelli's words, "to enact in our bodies what we proclaim with our lips."

There is more than a little irony in all this. Their beautiful building was constructed as a church for Cornelius Vanderbilt, the industrial baron of the Biltmore estate. The little gem of a church was originally conceived as a romantic English-style chapel, an exquisite worship space filled with arts and decor suiting the Vanderbilts' European tastes and refinement. Today, however, the people at All Souls insist that theirs is an inclusive community where the arts are "not the luxury of a few, but the best hope of humanity to experience joy on this planet." Art points the way to joy, the joy of touching the divine.

From the earliest days of Christianity, when new believers painted signs of their faith on the walls of Roman catacombs, art has pointed the way to God. Creativity is at the heart of every spiritually vital religious movement.

Sometimes, however, art can be contentious. Christians have long worried that the arts are so seductive that people might be tempted to worship the art or artist rather than the divine presence. So, Christian history is riddled with arguments over icons, paintings, stained glass windows, and statues. In some sad periods of the faith, Christian iconoclasts destroyed the beauties of the past. Today, that tendency is largely muted

– and Christians of all sorts are engaging the arts. However, there is still a rift in the ways that Christians view art. Some, usually those in evangelical churches, understand art instrumentally. Art is important because it proclaims a message, usually intended to convert people to the faith. Such congregations often offer elaborate Christmas or Easter programs, or put on religious plays or film series, with the sole purpose of convincing the audience to believe in Jesus. Art is important for what it can accomplish.

Other Christians, however, engage art for the sake of mystery instead of a message. Art reaches toward God, where humanity touches divinity, and where the intellectual fades to apprehending beauty. Art is important because it is a pathway of mystical experience with God. One Seattle Lutheran said that beauty "raises [people] out of the mundane, media-blitzed, cubical-induced lives that they live every day and somehow gives them a glimpse and hope of eternity." In Memphis a woman told me, "Part of what we do is theater. It is ritual and myth and things that are more important than anything...It is something that transcends the ever-changing world." As a California Presbyterian said bluntly about art, "It helps move people away from blind literalism: to what is 'truly there.'"

Although the arts are, indeed, mystical, they are not entirely ethereal. Throughout my journey, people taught me that beauty is a faith practice – something people do that can be learned, rehearsed, and enacted – in our lives and community. In their churches I saw art shows, artist studios, art programs for children, and summer art camps. There were piano lessons, artist seminars, book signings, poetry readings, and web design classes. From seniors to preschoolers, from the homeless to the prosperous, all sorts of people engaged the arts together. I saw ministers play guitar, do cartwheels, and dance. They wrote liturgies and composed hymns. In worship, they employed a range of arts – from traditional choirs singing to potters spinning, from painting icons to projecting PowerPoint images on walls. With only a few exceptions, their churches were elaborately decorated with candles, crosses, flowers, paintings, prints, pottery, banners, sculpture, weavings, embroidery, icons, and fountains. There were film series and craft workshops, knitting groups and drama troops. Liturgical dancers and shape-note singers. Madrigals and rock musicians. Most of it was good. All of it was done with heart. They made me think of Genesis: "And God saw everything that he had made, and indeed it was very good."

Of his congregation, Todd Donatelli said, "It is a community that believes that for those created in the image of God, a sign of their faithfulness, a sign of their engagement with the Spirit, will be creativity." Todd's observation held true in all the congregations along my way. They were a symphony of creativity! From them I learned that congregations can craft beauty through the arts, faithfully employing skills and gifts that opened the way toward helping them understand God beyond words. Through the arts, human beings embody God by imitating God's creative life – shaping the clay of their experience with voices and hands. In that place, everything becomes new as we participate in God's continual creation of the universe. Or, as one Congregationalist said of his renewed joy at being Christian, "I didn't realize it was so beautiful."

About the author

Diana Butler Bass (www.dianabutlerbass.com) is an author, speaker, and independent scholar specializing in American religion and culture. She holds a Ph.D. in religious studies from Duke University and is the author of six books, including the best-selling *Christianity for the Rest of Us*, which was named as one of the best religion books of the year by *Publishers Weekly* and *Christian Century*. She and her family live just outside of Washington, D.C.

1 Don E. Saliers, "Singing Our Lives," in *Practicing Our Faith*, ed. Bass, 182
2 Phyllis has told this story in a number of settings. She relates it in print in her *Prayer Is a Place: America's Religious Landscape Observed* (New York: Doubleday, 2005), 138–39
3 See Todd Donatelli, "Engaging Creativity," in *From Nomads to Pilgrims*, ed. Butler Bass and Stewart-Sicking

PART 1

Transforming Relationships
with God

The arts draw us deeply into the parts of ourselves where our most urgent questions and desires lodge. These desiring questions have as their source and end, God.
— Wendy M. Wright from "Potter and Clay: Thoughts on Forming and Being Formed" in March/April 2002 issue of Weavings: a Journal of the Christian Spiritual Life

The House of Love

Henri J. M. Nouwen

Hardly a day passes in our lives without our experience of inner or outer fears, anxieties, apprehensions, and preoccupations. These... powers have pervaded every part of our world to such a degree that we can never fully escape them. Still it is possible not to belong to these powers, not to build our dwelling place among them, but to choose the house of love as our home. This choice is made not just once and for all but by living a spiritual life, praying at all times and thus breathing God's breath. Through the spiritual life we gradually move from the house of fear to the house of love.

I have never seen the house of love more beautifully expressed than in the icon of the Holy Trinity, painted by Andrei Rublev in 1425 in memory of the great Russian saint, Sergius (1313–1392). For me the contemplation of this icon has increasingly become a way to enter more deeply into the mystery of divine life while remaining fully engaged in the struggles of our hate-and-fear-filled world.

Andrei Rublev painted this icon not only to share the fruits of his own meditation on the mystery of the Holy Trinity but also to offer his fellow monks a way to keep their hearts centered in God while living in the midst of political unrest. The more we look at this holy image with the eyes of faith, the more we come to realize that it is painted not as a lovely decoration for a convent church, not as a helpful explanation of a difficult doctrine, but as a holy place to enter and stay within. As we place ourselves in front of the icon in prayer, we come to experience a gentle invitation to participate in the intimate conversation that is taking place among the three divine angels and to join them around the table. The movement from the Father toward the Son and the movement of both Son and Spirit toward the Father become a movement in which the one who prays is lifted up and held secure.

During a hard period of my life in which verbal prayer had become nearly impossible and during which mental and emotional fatigue had made me the easy victim of feelings of despair and fear, a long and quiet presence to this icon became the beginning of my healing. As I sat for long hours in front of Rublev's Trinity, I noticed how gradually my gaze became a prayer. This silent prayer slowly made my inner restlessness melt away and lifted me up into the circle of love, a circle that could not be broken by the powers of the world. Even as I moved away from the icon and became involved in the many tasks of everyday life, I felt as if I did not have to leave the holy place I had found and could dwell there whatever I did or wherever I went. I knew that the house of love I had entered has no boundaries and embraces everyone who wants to dwell there.

About the author

Henri J. M. Nouwen was a Dutch Catholic priest who authored over 40 books on the spiritual life. After two decades of teaching in various academic settings (Menninger Foundation Clinic, University of Notre Dame, Yale University, Harvard University), he moved to the L'Arche community of Daybreak in Toronto, Ontario, and made his home there. He died in September of 1996.

Cooperative Endeavor with the Spirit

Richard J. Berryman

I had thought of icons as akin to stained-glass windows: more ancient, formalized and mysterious, perhaps, but simply an Eastern visual aid to devotion and understanding, equivalent to those glass pictures with which we Western Christians are so familiar. But my ideas changed when I took part in an intense icon writing retreat at the Anglican Monastery in Cambridge, Massachusetts. The spiritual impact that came from those days was truly staggering.

It was as if a deep spiritual presence within the icon writing process called up and echoed realities of the Spirit already hidden within me, waiting to be stirred into new life. I recalled Psalm 42, *One deep calls to another.* To one accustomed only to Western spirituality, it was strangely mystical.

It began when I started to etch the lines of the design into the surface of the icon board with a sharp-pointed metal stylus. What had been up to that moment only beloved words from Scripture suddenly became an experience.

I knew first-hand that I was carved into the hand of God. At an almost frighteningly profound level, I participated in a beautifully intimate image from the Book of Revelation. We are told there that when the faithful finally stand in the Presence of God, each will be handed a little white stone on which is carved the pet "nickname" by which God has known us since even before we were born. These were no longer familiar verbal texts and metaphors. I had entered into the mystery of their truth. It wasn't that I understood those images any better. It was that I now seemed, somehow, to have participated in them.

The next step was to paint a thin coating of red clay around the edge of the board and over the space that would eventually be the halo representing the divine life and spirit. The name *Adam* in the Genesis creation story is a form of the Hebrew word for red clay. The red clay of our humanity. The stuff of the earth and of our earthly nature.

Then, with deep breaths, we emptied our lungs closely onto the surface of the space filled with dull red clay, moistening it, preparing it. Onto the breath-moistened clay we placed 23-carat gold leaf, as thin as a human hair. When we lifted the protective backing from the gold it clung to the clay, transforming it, for the one who applied it, suddenly and stunningly into something more than mere symbol.

This moment, a moment that will clearly live long with me, is perhaps the most difficult part of the experience to convey. The spiritual effect of breathing "life" into that space on an icon's surface reduced me, and others, to tears of awe. Somehow I had encountered the One who calls each of us from the red clay of the earth to the potential of transformation into the divine image. I began to realize why the theology of Orthodox iconography is based on the transfiguration... It is a process of transformation not only of a painted image but also of the person who makes it, or uses it in prayer.

In applying the paint, each area is covered with dark tones to begin and successive applications of lighter colour are added, in some areas as many as eight layers. The movement is always from dark to light. There is a deepening sense that you are involved in an ongoing participation in the creative activity of the Holy Spirit. You are brooding over the chaos and continuing to bring design out of it, to bring light out of darkness.

This sense is heightened by the way in which the colours are applied. The brush does not touch the surface of the icon. The paint (which is ground up earth material) is very watery. As the iconographer, you "float" the colours onto the icon. With your brush you move only the surface of the water over the space you wish to colour into life. The "face of the water" settles, the water recedes by evaporation and the earth-based colours appear.

The verbal scriptural imagery we read in Genesis becomes an inner spiritual encounter and reality. It felt as if I was involved in a cooperative endeavor with the Creator Spirit, brooding and moving over the face of the deep. As a commentary on the Seventh Ecumenical Council says, "Liturgic art is not only our offering to God, but also God's descent into our midst, one of the forms in which is accomplished the meeting of God with [humanity], of grace with nature, eternity with time."

About the author

Archdeacon Richard Berryman during his professional life has been a parish pastor; the media director of the Anglican Church of Canada; a TV producer and host at CFPL in London, Ontario; the religion columnist of the Hamilton Spectator; and the Canon Missioner of a Cathedral. He is a Fellow of the College of Preachers in Washington, DC, and has published four books.

Taizé Journey

Doris Kizinna

With you, oh God, is life in all its fullness, and in your
light we shall seek new life.
~ TAIZÉ SONG

I boarded a train in Germany, full of anticipation – I was navigating the European train system in search of the small village of Taizé in the Burgundy region of France. It was the first time I had traveled completely on my own. I was 26 and the year was 1996. I was seeking a connection to my own spirit and to God's presence, all the while asking questions about my life and purpose. Who was this God my life was somehow bound to? Did this God even really exist? I needed to step away from the traditional and enter into a time of deep seeking. In the end, this journey to Taizé would enable me to return to the Christian faith as the place where I found direction, peace and connection with the Divine.

I arrived in Mâcon after a few train changes, and somehow found the city bus that would take me to Taizé. Tired from my night travels, I dimly watched the gorgeous rolling hills of this region of France through the bus window. The bus stopped in Cluny; then it came to Taizé, and I was let out at the bottom of a hill. I looked up and saw a few stone houses and an old stone church. Was this the place I had anticipated so much? It was still and quiet, a peaceful summer morning. How could a community of brothers that welcomes thousands of young people a week over the summer be up there?

I walked up the hill, and came closer to some of the ancient stone houses. I walked past a field of sunflowers, and enjoyed the hollyhocks in full bloom along the side of the road. I passed the village church, and found myself wondering where the heck this Taizé community was! As I reached the crest of the hill, a small universe unfolded: simple buildings; undercover areas; small benches scattered everywhere; a few circus-like tents in the distance; a long, low white building; groups of people here and there; and a big sign directing pilgrims to the welcome area. I followed the sign and was warmly welcomed by an enthusiastic greeter and one of the brothers who was preparing materials for new arrivals. I was given a place to sleep, an orientation to the schedule of Taizé, and then they asked me to pay for my stay: $21 for the week. What a deal!

As I walked out of the welcome building on my way to find my accommodation, bells began to ring, loudly and beautifully. I looked up and noticed a huge bell tower. I stood underneath and let the sound soak its way through me. I was enveloped by sound. People around me were starting to move toward the low white building. I looked at my watch – it was time for mid-day prayers. I made my way through a dusty open area, noticing people who held signs at the door: "Silence." I walked through the door, and entered a small universe of simple beauty.

The design and aesthetics of the church were the first things that drew me in. Warm lighting illuminated a central simple altar with large pieces of red fabric rising up to the ceiling. There were small clusters of candles around large icons, and the community was seated on the carpeted floor or on small wooden benches along the walls. I was mesmerized when the white-robed community of brothers entered the church, taking their places on the floor with the rest of the pilgrims, everyone facing toward the front of the church. It was like no place I had ever been before.

Then came the music. So simple, so clear, so deeply grounding. A single voice leading, and those gathered sharing in the repetitive chanting. A guitar, a flute would join in – each sound rising into a harmonious balance. The chanting would go on for five minutes or longer. Again, I was enveloped by sound – and again, I let sound soak into my soul. It was easy to get caught up in the songs, singing the same two lines over and over. The words became a mediation, deeply etching themselves into my mind and soul. Even today, I can sing any Taizé song by heart. They will not leave me.

There were over 4,000 people in the church for that mid-day worship. We sang together, observed silence together, and prayed together with Brother Roger leading us. I sat, taking it all in, deeply grateful for the sense of peace I was encountering. I do have to admit that I also wondered how I could possibly sit on the hard floor for over three hours a day for the next ten days! Even so, as I left the church following that first worship I could not wait until the longer evening service would begin, and once again, I could be enfolded in the beauty of the space and the song.

In the next ten days, I would attend over 30 Taizé worship services and spend three days in silence. I would sit in the church well into the night, with brothers and sisters from around the world, praying and yearning for answers to what I was seeking. All the while, I was singing. I spent time helping to set up some of the worship space before the services, placing candles and lights, and preparing the church. All the while, I was singing. I embraced a simple life for ten days – simple meals, simple accommodation, simple open connection with others – and all the while, I was singing. I was singing for all that I had sought and all that I had found in this small village on the top of a hill where community, reconciliation, and communion with God are bound together.

The impact of my experience at Taizé has shadowed my life in the years that have followed. It took a while for all that I had learned and been nourished by to enter deeply into my awareness and be integrated into my life. I arrived at that small village as a seeker, full of questions and doubt. Through the contemplative music and through my own personal communion with the Divine, I came to have some direction around my sense of belonging and about my life's purpose. After seeking God in places other than the Christian faith, I walked down that hill knowing that I had come back to the place where my life was mysteriously connected to the life of Jesus. In Taizé, I became a Lover of God and a singer of songs.

I returned to my life in Canada, knowing that I would take seriously the brothers' call to take the experience of Taizé and live it in my own context. I began a Taizé service in the congregation I served in as youth minister, deeply valuing setting up the space, as I had in Taizé, and providing a place for people to experience the simple experience of song, prayer and silence. In 2004, I took a group of young adults from Canada to Taizé for a week. I lead workshops and Taizé services regularly in my ministry.

The songs of Taizé continue to sustain me. Often, as I'm going about my day, a Taizé chant will come to me and I will start to sing. I remember that those who are gathered in Taizé are singing these same songs every day without fail, and I feel connected to them. It is with deep gratitude that I remember the place that gently called me back to where I belong.

About the author

Doris Kizinna is an artist, a writer, a youth minister, an extravagant cook, a seeker, and a lover of God who strives to create spaces of community, care, and beauty where all are welcomed. Doris has made her own pilgrimage to Taizé three times in her life so far, and sings the songs of Taizé as part of her spiritual practice. Doris is working on an upcoming book, *Go Deep: Spiritual Practices for Youth*, to be published in Spring 2009 by CopperHouse, an imprint of Wood Lake Publishing, Inc.

To find out more about the Taizé community: www.taize.fr

Creating Change

Taking Flight

Melissa Richeson-O'Neil

© Melissa Richeson-O'Neil

I have often joked that I must have been born at church. I was what our church nursery workers called a "cradle roll" baby, which I figure should rank right up there near "founding member."

One of my earliest memories is of the church nursery where I spent so many hours. It was an old, high ceilinged room, and its contents included two of my favorite things in all the world: rocking horses and swings. I loved to gallop into oblivion on the rocking horses whenever I had the chance, but the swings seemed extraordinary to me. They were daring – their cloth harnesses hung way down from the tall ceilings, providing for the ultimate in motion. I would have happily swung in them forever. When the nursery ladies would strap me in a swing and patiently begin to push me, I would launch into the heavens...or so I thought. I flew in those swings, and each flight seemed to free something within me. It was as though I moved into another realm of being, and nothing but the flight mattered.

Now, many years later, I think about those hours I spent flying to another realm in the church nursery swing, and in the same instant, I recall learning the Hebrew word *ruach*. *Ruach* – even the sound of it conveys the *wind*, the *spirit*, the *breath* of its meaning – God breathing life into me at the moment of my creation. *Whoosh!* I can hear the breath even now. Flying in that swing carried me back to the place of wonder – the place where I was open and filled with God's spirit, with *ruach*.

Between those two epiphanies, life took over: school, travel, teaching, and marriage. I lived in different places, attended different churches – it was all more or less a routine.

And then, in my mid thirties, I walked into a small church in the heart of Texas and noticed things were "different." The ministers were decked out in robes...and stoles...and one Sunday, members changed the cloths on the communion table from one color to another. My eyes were riveted. One morning, just as December was coming, I walked into the sanctuary and was mesmerized by a ten-foot long banner of rich fabric and design hanging at the front of the worship space. Other huge banners hung on the side walls, each seemingly more exquisite than the last. A lone voice from the back sang a plaintive verse of *O Come, O Come, Emmanuel*, and shivers ran down my spine. I began hearing a child's footsteps breaking the silence, and I watched spellbound as she purposely strode forward and lit one lone candle peering from a wreath of evergreens. The service began. I had just been given my first taste of Advent.

Once again, there was *ruach*, God filling me with God's spirit. *Whoosh!* I can almost hear my lungs and mind and soul expanding in welcome even now. So began my discovery of and ever increasing wonder and fascination with the seasons of the church year. Possibilities of visuals for all the liturgical celebrations began dancing within me. Despite my years of teaching art and sewing anything and everything, I had never considered possible connections between my creative side and my faith. The concept seemed equally terrifying and liberating. It also felt extremely radical to me, the Southern Baptist cradle roll kid!

I began volunteering my artistic skills for church-bulletin boards, theatre scenery, and illustrations. Church members showered my efforts with unbridled enthusiasm, welcoming each new project with joy and requests for more. I was astounded by all the positive responses, and truly looked forward to each creative opportunity that came to me.

In time, I moved to another town and another church. But the seed planted within me that first Advent had germinated. I began to design and create banners for my new church. In retrospect, I was pretty clueless about the traditional symbolism and nuances of each liturgical season, but I worked with the confidence that each finished piece would be beautiful.

During the process, it happened again – the *whoosh* of *ruach*. I'd be cutting fabric, trying out colors, having little conversations like: "Hey, God…what do you think about this color here?" It was as though time stopped, the universe stopped, and all that mattered at that moment was God and me, and our interaction. I remember watching my work develop as though I was on the outside, my eyes tracking the motions of my hands with amazement and incredulity. I was in another realm, and nothing else mattered. I was hooked.

I enrolled in a master's program to study liturgical arts. (*Liturgical* was a new word for me. I would throw it out in conversation and watch people stare at me like I had just named some new and terrible disease.) During my coursework, I was blessed to intern with an extremely talented fabric artist well known for her liturgical work. I rated my attempts feeble in comparison, but I absorbed as much of her wisdom as I could. During the last weeks of my coursework, however, I began to grow anxious. Seminary friends were celebrating their new church assignments while I had no plan of action for the future. So, I asked God to answer my queries for direction via a gigantic billboard. I figured that such a message would be too obvious for me to misinterpret the meaning. The month before graduation, ten unsolicited fabric commissions came my way – all from local congregations. If that did not qualify as a billboard from heaven, nothing would. I bought a new sewing machine and turned my spare bedroom into a studio. Then, it was pedal to the metal!

My first pieces included a pallium for one of my professors (who claimed she felt like a bishop when wearing it!) and the ordination stole for a dear friend. Many times I felt like I was sewing through days and nights of my life. Bits and pieces of threads seemed to cling to me, and I still joke about my "trail of threads." One church commissioned me to create a pulpit piece for every season of the church year. Luckily, my friend was a member there, and more importantly, she was entrusted with a key to the building. In the early days, I was not always adept at estimating my work schedule. Sometimes, I was crunching drastically close to deadlines. On a few occasions, out of sheer necessity, we would meet at the church in the wee hours of the morning to install a piece before anyone assembled to begin preparing for worship. Yet, those moments in the dark and empty worship space became holy treasures for both of us. In the space of that hallowed ground, stark in its echoing emptiness, *ruach* would fill me once more. It was a time to offer up the work of my hands for the blessing of my Creator.

I've been privileged to create a number of pieces for Advent Lutheran Church, an ELCA community in Columbus, Ohio. I love worshipping at Advent, absorbing the space, the music and the people into my being. Four dedicated church committee members have continued to work with me through the years, toiling tirelessly through many projects, always conveying their love of worship with me. They come to our meetings brimming with information and ideas.

A couple of years ago, we met to bounce around ideas for Pentecost/Reformation pieces, and an in-depth discussion began about the color red: blood red, fire red, this red and that red. As usual, these four human wonders threw so many ideas at me that my head was swimming. How could all the ideas work together? How could they be combined without visual overload? I listened, took copious notes, and drew strength from the prayer which had opened the meeting for me. I had prayed for direction and guidance, to be open for use as God's instrument. The meeting ended with all of us jokingly wondering aloud where our ideas would go.

Where did the ideas go? Straight to heaven, I think, because they rushed back down as a cohesive and wondrous design. When wind, fire, a star-inspired cross, the dove of the Holy Spirit, palms of celebration – all the pertinent themes – suddenly came together, alive in one piece, I was astounded. I was smiling uncontrollably when we reconvened to look at the design. Jane, who always impresses me with her commitment and research, almost cried as saw her dreams in a visible form. She told me she never understands how I can work with all the ideas that are voiced at our brainstorming sessions. I never hesitated when I told her, "Jane, I did not do this. God did. I was honored to experience the miracle."

The designing of a piece continues to be gut-wrenching, tear-inducing, and divine. I know those words sound like an exercise in contrasts. I always gather ideas from my clients, research, and files of visual stimuli before I start to sketch. Yet sometimes, when I sit down with pencil and paper, it seems impossible to make any indelible mark, much less develop a cohesive design. Erasures litter my work area as the frustration level mounts. The divine part comes, seemingly unbidden at times, when I finally let go of my pre-conceived ideas and let *ruach* fill me once more. I feel God flow into and through me, and my hands seem to move across design work, leaving lines I could never have imagined. I'm filled with awe as I watch the process unfold – as colors announce their positions and threads create their patterns.

I become lost in the wonder and mystery of the creative act itself, and once again, I am flying high, in another realm of being. Once again, *ruach* fills me. My entire being delights in the breath of the Creator God. I am open and God is in me, God creating me in God's image.

Whoosh!

No other flight compares.

About the author

Melissa Richeson-ONeil is a fabric artist whose work has enhanced churches from Lutheran, Presbyterian, United Church of Christ, and Catholic traditions. She majored in Fine Art and Education at the University of Dallas and the University of North Texas. After graduation, she taught art in the Caribbean as Peace Corps volunteer and contract teacher. Upon completion of her Master of Arts in Liturgical Arts at the Methodist Theological School in Ohio, she opened up her working studio, Locusts & Honey (www.locustsandhoney.com).

Tuning the E String

Barbara Brown Taylor

A man I know raised four children with few requirements of them. But one of those few was that each of them learn to play a musical instrument. This would not only supply them with discipline and delight, he reasoned. It would also give the family a language that surpassed speech, and his children a patois that would carry them around the world.

My parents had roughly the same idea, except that my piano lessons were strictly for my own improvement. No one else in the family played anything, and the only person I had to commune with was Mrs. Blitch, my piano teacher, who set her metronome with all the gravity of an inquisitor positioning her rack. After I failed to show any promise at the piano, I was introduced to the flute, the clarinet and the guitar, in that order. The fact that my parents rented those instruments told me everything I needed to know about their confidence in my ability. When I went off to college, I went without so much as a kazoo in my trunk.

Somewhere along the way I fell in love with a young man who made mountain dulcimers. Under his spell, I bought a two-octave psaltery made from polished blond wood and learned to tease simple tunes from it with a dainty horsehair bow. With that lovely instrument perched on my lap, I felt positively biblical. I sang psalms. I played hymns. I made things up. When the romance ended, so did the music. I got a job. I got busy. I put the psaltery on a shelf.

Last week I took it down again, at least partly because I had just watched an 88-year-old woman blow a mean tune on her two-sided Marine Band harmonica. Her face was gray when she started out and pink when she finished. The transformation was so total that I decided I could not afford to age any further without music in my life.

The psaltery was parked on a high shelf in the ironing room. When I pulled the bow from the case, half of the horsehairs swung loose in the breeze. The psaltery itself looked no worse for my neglect of it, except that the strings had all stretched out of shape. Starting with the low E, I blew on a pitch pipe and set the bow to the string, twisting the peg so that the sound went above the note and then below.

At first I did not know that the music was inside of me. I kept blowing the pipe, bowing the string and twisting the peg, without enough hands to manage it all. Finally I tried humming the note, holding it while I stretched the string this way and that. The discord made my jaws ache. Then the string found E and my whole body agreed. The note inside of me and the note outside of me were the same note. There could be no doubt.

Since I live with a lot of doubt, this tuning of the E string had a large effect on me. After long years of seeking certainty about things that cannot be seen, I have pretty much surrendered to the necessity of faith: that love will last, that goodness has power, that God is real. I cannot lay hands on any of these things any more than I can hold an E note up by its stem.

There are whole months, in fact, when both faith and music seem like impossible luxuries. What kind of music can a child from Sierra Leone make, with raw stumps where her hands once were? Would anyone like to address the Joint Chiefs of Staff on the power of goodness? I suspect that I am not the only person who ever put her psaltery on a shelf because its small clear voice sounded irreverent against the vast groaning of the world.

The discovery that E exists independently of my faith in it is no small thing. Even when I am not searching for it, the note is there. I cannot say where "there" is, exactly, since it is no place I can see, but when I hear the note I know it. I furthermore know that I did not create it. It was real before I ever was and it will remain real long after I am gone. Its reality is such that no one has to take my word for it, either. When I stretch the string just right and set the bow to it, I make a sound that has a name. Any stranger with a good enough ear can walk by and say, "That's an E."

The trustworthiness of this note makes up for its smallness. While I am learning to find it on a more reliable basis, it waits patiently to be found. It is not going anywhere, because time means nothing to it. It has always been E and it will always be E. It has all the time in the world. Twisting the string peg this way and that, I set loose sounds that make those around me wince. Apparently I am not the only one who suffers from my disharmony. But when I find the note at last, there are no words for the pleasure of the reunion. There is only the music, as the E inside of me and the E outside of me round into one. Is it my imagination, or is the pleasure mutual? I would testify under oath that the note was as glad to be found as I was to find it.

Perhaps this is the gift my friend wanted to give his four children, as well as the one my parents wanted to give me: the early assurance that there is an enduring harmony as certain as the groaning of the world, whose small clear voice is the truest one of all. Rather late in my life, I have taken this promise off the shelf. God willing, I shall play with all the time I have left.

About the author

Barbara Brown Taylor teaches religion at Piedmont College in Demorest, Georgia, where she holds the Harry R. Butman Chair in Religion and Philosophy. She also serves as adjunct professor of Christian spirituality at Columbia Theological Seminary in Decatur, Georgia. Taylor is the author of eleven books.

Revealing New Signs

Thomas Merton

If these drawings are able to persist in a certain autonomy and fidelity, they may continue to awake possibilities, consonances; they may dimly help to alter one's perceptions. Or they may quietly and independently continue to invent themselves. Such is the "success" they aspire to. Doubtless there is more ambition than modesty in such an aim. For the only dream a man seriously has when he takes a brush in his hand and dips it into ink is to reveal a new sign that can continue to stand by itself and to exist in its own right, transcending all logical interpretation.

– Notebook 14, 1964, Thomas Merton Center collection

The peculiar quality of Chinese and Japanese art that is influenced by Zen is that it is able to suggest what cannot be said, and, by using a bare minimum of form, to awaken us to the formless. Zen painting tells us just enough to alert us to what is *not* and is nevertheless "right there." Zen calligraphy, by its peculiar suppleness, dynamism, abandon, contempt for "prettiness" and for formal "style," reveals to us something of the freedom which is not transcendent in some abstract and intellectual sense, but which employs a minimum of form without being attached to it, and is therefore free from it.

– Zen and the Birds of Appetite

The genius of the artist finds its way by the affinity of creative sympathy, or conaturality, into the living law that rules the universe. This law is nothing but the secret gravitation that draws all things to God as to their center. Since all true art lays bare the action of this same law in the depths of our own nature, it makes us alive to the tremendous mystery of being, in which we ourselves, together with all other living and existing things, come forth from the depths of God and return again to [God].

– No Man Is an Island

About the author

Thomas Merton (1915–1968) was a writer and Trappist monk at Our Lady of Gethsemani Abbey in Kentucky. He wrote over 70 books during his lifetime, including personal journals, poetry, collections of letters, social criticism, and writings on peace, justice, and ecumenism.

PART 2

Transforming Communities

*Art points out the beauty we might otherwise miss,
as well as the injustices we might otherwise dismiss.*
– Bob Hulteen, Popular Culture and our Future

Caroling with the Homeless

Jim Strathdee

It was a cold and blustery Northern California day in late December. Jean and I stood with mandolin and guitar, leading Christmas carols in Friendship Park, a place of hospitality for Sacramento's homeless people. A friend of ours and minister-at-large to the homeless community had asked us to go caroling with his flock. We held a quick and shivering rehearsal in the chilly midmorning and, then, about thirty of us decided to go caroling together. Huddled in vans, we set off to our first stop: the Sacramento County Building, where the supervisors were discussing a proposal to build one thousand low-income cottages for homeless families. We hoped that our songs of peace and goodwill might affect public policy (those who had ears to hear). We went on to sing to the people in the nearby state and federal buildings. This begins the heart of what I want to share with you.

I found this to be an amazing, eye-opening and heart-changing experience. These thirty rag-tagged residents of our city's streets and shelters sang with a gusto and fervor that deeply moved me. Seeing the old carols through their eyes gave the words a new meaning to me, even though some of the words were changed: "I'm dreaming of a *warm* Christmas." "Away in a manger no crib for a bed" was especially poignant.

But what was more amazing to me was the response of the bureaucrats and office workers that keep our government going. Although it was very evident where this group of singers came from, they were seen, acknowledged and received – an experience all too rare. Many of us middle-class professionals would prefer that "these people" remain invisible, but the dress and demeanor of homelessness is difficult to disguise. What the office people found hard to believe was that "these people" who had so little themselves were offering to others songs of Christmas love with obvious joy and dignity.

At one point, we stood on a second-story balcony encircling a large rotunda. Many workers had come out of their offices on the far side of the balcony to hear us sing. We rendered our full repertoire, with carols bouncing off the marbled halls and rotunda as though in a cathedral. Songs of God's reign: hope, longing, justice and heavenly peace! Across the way, handkerchiefs came out of pockets, tissue out of purses, unexpected tears were wiped away. After our final song, there was an echo of silence and we all just looked at each other across the cavernous space. In that moment I knew a great gulf had been bridged. I knew that we stood in the presence of that heavenly peace we so long for and sing about. For a moment we were there!

The old carols still can unify our diverse culture in song and vision. But it was the context of bringing together people in the center of authority and those on the margin of society that gave these familiar carols their power that day. I am very clear that it will take more than singing to make peace and good will a social reality. But when the context and the music are aligned, we can glimpse wholeness and Shalom for a moment, and celebrate its presence among us.

It *is* God's world, God's realm. God's ways are the only viable option for a sustainable and vital existence on our planet. God's Kin-dom is *already here* waiting for us to choose and affirm it with our acts of courage and understanding, compassion, and justice. God's Spirit is always with us, luring us and leading us into "Kin-dom moments." Our challenge is to be open to see, hear, and sense God's presence at every turn – then take the risk to trust the Spirit's song, dance and journey for our lives. In this time of great confusion over religious language, the Spirit is speaking loudly to us through the arts. Music, dance, drama, prose, poetry, cinema, and all the visuals arts can help us reconnect to our deepest selves and to God's intention for the entire human family and all of creation.

It was a rare and beautiful gift for my homeless friends and the government office workers to truly *see* and *hear* each other that day. Through our shared music, eyes and ears were opened, hearts were tenderized, and we knew the ground on which we stood was holy...and I'm happy to report that the 1,000 cottages were built.

Keep the faith, my friends! Keep on singing! God's peace to you!

About the authors

Composers and singers, Jim and his wife, Jean, have shared their music in an international itinerant ministry for over thirty-five years, offering concerts, leading worship celebrations, and serving as conference song and choral leaders. Their music brings hope and encouragement to faith communities actively seeking peace, justice, and healing in God's world.

Over the years, the Strathdees have served as music directors in several United Methodist congregations, most recently for sixteen years at St. Mark's in Sacramento. They are now devoting their time to writing, publishing, recording, and traveling to sing. Their music is published in dozens of songbooks, curriculum projects, denominational hymnbooks, and supplements. For more information go to www.strathdeemusic.com.

Into the Heart of the Other
Interfaith Story Circles

Gert Johnson

I stepped into storytelling thirteen years ago. During my graduate studies in theology I wrote a master's thesis on the use of storytelling in moral education with adolescents, documenting my work using this approach with my high school religious studies classes. This experience literally transformed my teaching and left me longing for further knowledge and experimentation with story.

Members of the local guild of the National Storytelling Network (NSN) were my first mentors in storytelling. I learned much from attending their circles. However, their emphasis was on telling stories with an eye to professional performance. I dreamed of a circle where the focus would be on stories of faith and spirituality – stories that could be a source of revelation, inspiration, and possible transformation in everyday life. This circle would be composed of peoples of different faiths, bringing the riches of their story traditions to the table, recognizing the value of our diverse truths and those we hold in common.

My dream became a reality in 1993. There were just three of us at that first circle. During the next four years we met at a fixed place, our circle remaining small in size and scope and top-heavy with Christian tellers and listeners. Looking back on that time, I am reminded of the parable of the mustard seed and of the uncommon grace God can give us to have faith and persevere in the face of things "not yet seen."

This past September, Interfaith Story Circle celebrated its tenth anniversary at an interfaith sanctuary in Albany, New York. We are now a storytelling group made up of people of many faiths, a real mix of professional tellers and those who come simply out of a love for story. Our circles meet monthly from September to June, each hosted by a different faith community and led by a storyteller with expertise in a particular area. The teller spends a bit of time sharing his/her knowledge and a few stories on that month's theme. Then the circle is open for all to tell. No one need plan or sign up to tell. We simply allow the stories to move and inspire us, to take us where they will.

Each circle begins and ends with prayer and runs for two hours. There is no break. None is needed. One story begets another, catching us up and carrying us along. We are often reluctant to see our time together come to an end. After the circle, we leaf through theme-related books that the teller has brought, pick up the provided list of resources, and linger a bit. As lights are dimmed, doors are closed, and people head home, one can still hear bits of stories being exchanged, floating up into the night sky.

The week before our anniversary circle I spent some time alone in the sanctuary. Sitting beneath the round stained glass windows, their vividly swirling blues portraying the energy of creation and of interfaith dialogue, I scanned a list of our past circles. One after another I drew them up in my mind's eye, picturing the sacred spaces where we gather: Catholic, Episcopal, Methodist, Presbyterian, and Reformed churches, Jewish synagogues and temples, a local Buddhist center, and the Hindu temple and Muslim mosque that will host us this spring. I reflected on the variety and richness of our times together: evenings of tales from the various faith traditions; circles sharing stories of death and dying, bereavement, suffering, and reconciliation; our yearly gathering of teens telling tales; circles focused on telling our own stories for discernment, prayer, and spiritual enrichment; and those that have explored the use of storytelling in liturgy and ministry.

One after another, I remembered stories that had been told. One after another, I silently thanked the tellers who had led these circles, those who had come to listen, and those who felt prompted to tell in return. They are the people who have helped Interfaith Story Circle grow from the mustard seed it once was into the tree with many branches it is today.

A week later, as we gathered in the sanctuary, circling around our "spiritual fire" to celebrate ten years of telling, many of the same people were present in person, and they spoke readily of what Interfaith Story Circle has meant to them.

Marni, an accomplished teacher/teller/coach and author of books on storytelling, spoke of how she was "shy" at first to speak of her faith in any public way; of how having her stories welcomed and honored in Interfaith Circle has not only enabled her to share her personal journeys of faith but also has spilled over into her work in prison ministry and with troubled teens, helping those people to do the same.

Waynet, a student at a local graduate school of theology and ministry, told of coming to story circle last year to help satisfy the school's requirement for practical experience in ministry. She spoke enthusiastically of her first time with us, of hearing a minister "storytell Matthew's dry and boring genealogy of Jesus" in a way that awakened her to "the power story has to bring Scripture and theology to life."

Anne remembered how she first came to story circle intending to be a listener but soon felt compelled to tell. "Telling in circle has opened me up and given me the courage to share this gift in my faith community," she said. Anne recently portrayed the biblical character Elizabeth in her storytelling of the angel Gabriel's visitation. Her fellow parishioners' enthusiastic response prompted her to consider more tellings of women in Scripture.

Joe, a producer of many story events in our area, reminisced about the more formal Advent, Winter Lights, and Lenten tellings we have held in the broader community. Joe was instrumental in moving us in this direction, encouraging us to include free-will offerings to benefit food pantries and homeless shelters as part of these programs, adding a service dimension to our community tellings. Kate, who is not a member of any faith tradition, shared her own experience at Winter Lights. "I came feeling out of kilter," she said. "Being welcomed and hearing the stories brought peace to my spirit. And seeing the Advent wreath, the menorah, and the lights of the Hindu tradition on the altar, all coexisting, gave me a sense that we are all part of the Light."

I spoke of a member who could not be with us at the celebration: twelve-year-old Adah, a naturally gifted teller who often comes with her mother to circle and delights us with her stories. With coaching, she has summoned the courage to tell tales from her Jewish tradition at two Winter Lights programs. Adah's presence is motivating us to work at making our circle truly intergenerational.

Mussarat spoke of having been invited to come to our evening of Muslim tales not long after 9/11. She had hesitated, she explained, because "it was a time when people were suspicious of Muslims"; she was also a bit skeptical because the facilitator had a non-Muslim name. Her feelings changed during the circle, however, as she realized that the people who told that night had worked hard to find very special stories rooted in her tradition.

Her recollection brought that evening back to me. People were gathering in the circle as Mussarat and her three friends entered the sanctuary. We welcomed them, asking them to "come join the circle." With smiles and nods they took their places, replying "Thank you, but we've just come to listen, not to tell." We assured them that was fine. After prayer, Carol, our facilitator, shared her research on storytelling in the Islamic tradition, then told a tale she had prepared. "Oh, my father told me that story when I was a little girl," Mussarat remarked. She went on to explain the spiritual significance of the hajj (pilgrimage), which figures in this tale, and gave a wonderfully moving account of her last trip to Mecca. After Carol's next story, one of Mussarat's friends said, "I know that story, but my version is a bit different," and she shared hers with us.

One after another, our storytellers offered Muslim tales, and the Muslim women responded in kind. "Ah, the stories are wielding their power," I thought – breaking down barriers, opening minds and hearts to share.

Mussarat concluded her anniversary remembrance by saying, "Of all the interfaith activities I have been involved in over the years, this seems to be the one that gets to your heart. You can really feel each other's spiritualities."

And on and on the sharing went. We videotaped our anniversary circle, and I will show the tape this summer as part of a presentation at the National Storytelling Conference. Many storytellers around the country – some of them members of NSN's new interfaith discussion group and listserv – have expressed an interest in forming interfaith circles in their communities. These tellers are sharing and encouraging my current dream: that one day there will be interfaith story circles such as ours scattered throughout our country, perhaps throughout the world.

About the author

Gert Johnson, a member of St. John the Baptist Church in Schenectady, New York, is the founder and coordinator of Interfaith Story Circle of the Tri-City Area. She is a retired 30-year teacher of religious studies, a presenter of workshops on the use of storytelling for religious education and creative church ministry at the local and national levels, and a teller of tales in classroom and spiritual settings.

Words to Live By

Elizabeth Maxwell

What has the writers workshop meant for you?" I asked Joe. He has been a guest, and then a volunteer, at our soup kitchen for several years. He's been involved in the writing program for the last two. "Has it been a safe space?"

"Much more than a safe place!" Joe replied with some passion. "It has been more like a cauldron!"

This image of a cauldron – magician's brew, or maybe just a humble soup pot – strikes me as weirdly, wonderfully apt for a writing program in a soup kitchen. The participants bring to it their hunger to tell their stories, to find their voices, to learn a craft, to be heard. The stew of poetry and prose, honesty and courage, nourishes them as they share their work and hear and support their colleagues. In the mix, there can be alchemy, though like all alchemy it is impossible to say exactly how it happens or where its magic resides. People touch a place within them where something new comes into being, and, maybe, they change. Sometimes the world changes too. In any case, the world is richer for the stories that have come into it.

The workshop takes place at the Holy Apostles Soup Kitchen, the major outreach program of the Church of the Holy Apostles, an Episcopal parish in the Chelsea section of New York City. We're the largest emergency feeding program in Manhattan and in the Episcopal church nationally. We serve between 1,100 and 1,400 guests every weekday, mostly men but also women and children from infancy to 80 and beyond; African American, white, Latino; bike messengers; ex-offenders; guys in suits; long-term homeless, and folks who never imagined they'd stand on a soup kitchen line. They may be addicted or mentally ill, they may have had a catastrophic illness, a divorce, or just been unable to find a job over a long time. Whoever they are, we try – sometimes more successfully than others – to offer them hospitality in Christ's name, and to see Christ in them.

Ten years ago, the writer Ian Frazier came to me with the idea of starting a writer's workshop for our guests. That first day, sitting at a table near the church's exit door, he got more than 50 takers, each of whom told him about a story they wanted to write. A much smaller number actually showed up for the workshop, but somewhere between nine and 13 people sat together and wrote for about 40 minutes, and then read their writing to each other. Ian and co-teacher Bob Blaisdell wrote too. They proposed topics: shoes, how I came to New York, my first love, my worst day. Each week the writing was collected and typed, and at the end of the 10-week workshop, we produced an anthology. The workshop concluded with a public reading, and each participant read his or her favorite work. It was a resounding success.

The workshop has followed the same format every spring since, with other wonderful teachers getting involved along the way. Through the years a core group of writers has developed, and the stories they tell are heartfelt and often deeply moving. To their great, amazed delight, Seabury Press published *Food for the Soul*, a collection of their writings – one writer described seeing her work in print as "better than the best sex you've ever had." Anticipating publication, participant John Cabello penned a poem with these lines: "Let us meet next/Autumn at least at the park, in front of the building/When our book will be produced, as if to say/We are important, our lives a mystery that counts!"

For me, the workshop has been a revelation of that mystery. Initially I wasn't convinced our guests would commit to something as intangible as a writing program. I thought they would be too focused on their basic needs to be interested. What I learned, though, is that writing *is* a basic human need. It includes the need to count, to express oneself and be heard, to make sense of the life one has lived, to use one's imagination and language to make something new. Or, as Peter Nkruma put it in a piece called "Ten Rules for Living," "Create. How else will anyone know that you have been a part of life?"

In the first chapter of Genesis, God speaks the world into existence. God speaks wild words – galaxies, rivers, mountains, pine trees, whales, giraffes, hummingbirds – and is delighted with the result. By the time God gets around to creating humankind in God's own image, we have a picture of the divine as a profligate, playful artist of the word. Maybe one way human beings participate, not only in the community of creation but also in the divine mystery, is by creating as truly, skillfully, and passionately as we can. These writers bring order to chaos, name their experience, redeem loss and suffering through language, play with words, and delight in the realization that their work is good. Maybe the experience of creating has healing power in part because it opens us to the flow of the deep source of life within and joins us to something God is doing in the world. John Cabello's poem touches on this idea: "Whatever may happen – either beauty,/Ugliness or many times something undefined,/I see all of us, sharing verbs, words, the real/Root of God's spirit in us, longing to make work/Of high value."

The stories are unique and deeply universal at the same time. Some, raw and painful, seem particularly important because I don't hear them in many other places. One writer tells of being pulled out of the East River after an alcohol-driven suicide attempt. Another describes losing his job, falling behind in his rent, and moving to a homeless shelter – a bewildering place where mice crawled on his bed, a man died of an overdose in the bathroom down the hall, and the tables in the dining hall were too dirty to touch. A third writes of being raped in childhood and then reads his words aloud – the first time he's told the story to anyone. A woman tells about caring for her seriously ill son, and ultimately watching him die. Such stories, hard to bear, have stretched my heart and changed my understanding of the world I live in. I hope they change the way I live.

But many of the stories are also hilariously funny, deeply celebratory, or just plain quirky. They too are important. The talent in the writing is sometimes stunning, the courage even more so. I discover the challenges and struggles that poor people face in New York City, I realize the writers are so like me and utterly themselves, and I get a glimpse of the mystery that counts. The workshop's alchemy has revealed a richer, more complex human community than I had known about, a community in which we all participate, whether we know it or not, because we are connected in that mystery.

When I ask participants what this project has meant for them, they say community has been a central part of the experience. They value the feeling that everyone – teachers included – shares the struggles and thrills of getting their thoughts down on paper. Perhaps because writing is hard, risky work, a foundational sense of good will has prevailed. Joe tells me the workshop also has been spiritual for him – it has given him the discipline of writing every day, a practice he says "gets the junk out." Tory says writing "purges the pain and coalesces things, so then I can deal with them." Similarly, for Joe, the workshop challenged him to write the truth and then offered the possibility of having it heard – "you have to read what you might never tell anybody." Having done that, he says, you have to stand by your truth. It changes you.

Carol, a red-haired Southern woman who says that when she came to the workshop seven years ago she was "desperately hungry and creatively bankrupt," credits the writing program with helping her find hope. It also reawakened a dream she laid aside in high school, when a teacher told her, "I have other students who write much better than you do." After that, she never bothered to write again, until she saw a flyer for this workshop. Eventually Carol began to volunteer at the soup kitchen and met people who could tell her where to get other help she needed. "I found medical attention, both physical and mental. I was able to deal with some long-standing issues... It has been a long process, and I have not yet come full circle, but I'm almost there."

Many writers speak of "finding a voice" through the workshop – a voice that may be both creative and political. Joe, who had a serious heart attack several years ago, wrote about difficulties with his pharmacy. "When you get your feelings out, you learn you don't have to put up with things. This gave me a step up." He has begun to advocate for himself. Carol says she has begun to speak out on behalf of others too. "The workshop has made me speak out about [former NYC mayor Rudy] Giuliani and the soup kitchen, about political people and the poor. It has caused me to reflect and speak out on the Iraq war. What I think, now I have the voice to say it."

About the author

Elizabeth Maxwell has been associate rector of the Church of the Holy Apostles and program director of the Holy Apostles Soup Kitchen since 1989. As a spiritual director and retreat leader, she is interested in the relationship between the creative process, soul work, and social change.

Man of Sorrows

Catherine Kapikian

When an artist has a personal experience of the Christ of faith, he or she plumbs a deep reservoir from which to draw interpretive ideas. Several years ago a student [of Wesley Theological Seminary], named Maxwell Lawton, was hospitalized deathly ill. Diagnosed with AIDS, Maxwell's doctors gave him three months to live. Resolute despite ebbing strength, Maxwell insisted that his nurses disconnect his IV drips, enabling him to attend class on a day pass...Hours later, spent, he would reconnect.

Maxwell survived his death sentence and returned to seminary doggedly determined. For the next year and a half, he studied, watched his friends die, and coped with End-Stage AIDS. The enormity of his catastrophe overtook him in a solitary moment in his dorm room. Grief shook him to his core, consolable only as dawning awareness of Isaiah 53, a circulating text during this Advent time, seeped its way into his being. "He was despised and rejected by men; a man of sorrows and acquainted with grief..." Suddenly, Maxwell knew himself known and not alone.

A trained artist, Maxwell had found comfort and healing, he claims, working in the far corner of the seminary arts studio. There he started to paint what he was experiencing because he knew God's grief. Under his hand, a 36" by 42" canvas titled *Man of Sorrows: Christ with AIDS* sprung to life. Maxwell's Jesus, with a body racked by Kaposi's sarcoma lesions and tethered to an IV bottle and oxygen tank, wore a crown of thorns. Blanketed in a wash of subtly superimposed text from Matthew 25: "I was hungry...I was naked...I was sick...as you did it to one of the least of these...you did it to me," his Jesus challenged anyone willing to confront it. Maxwell's canvas talked back to the loud and shrill voices claiming that AIDS was a consequence of God's judgment upon those who deserved it.

Several years later, following repeated hospitalizations and countless drug interventions, Maxwell set off for Cape Town, South Africa. He went as a high-risk patient on an experimental oral medication to stave off impending blindness (CMV retinitis), a complication of AIDS. Ensconced in the back of St. George's Anglican Church for the month of December in 1994, Maxwell inaugurated AIDS awareness month at his easel with paints, palette, and brushes. His second and larger 4' by 6' *Man of Sorrows* sprang to life. It too was blanketed with superimposed text from Matthew 25, this time in Xhosa, Afrikaans, and English, the three languages spoken in Cape Town.

Uproar. A gathering momentum of people stormed the cathedral and demanded the painting's removal. Members of the majority population, decimated by the disease, rejoiced in Maxwell's Jesus. While his adversaries spit on him and yelled at him, others cried in the presence of the painting. They thanked him and gave him gifts, sometimes with the whisper, "Don't recognize me in the street." The stigma of AIDS crucified. Cafes buzzed. Radio commentators chattered. When Maxwell's life was threatened, he was put under cathedral custody. Newspaper reporters and television commentators companioned the crowds circling the cathedral.

The cathedral's board of trustees convened. They could not agree as to where to place the painting. Archbishop Desmond Tutu was recruited. He stepped up and agreed that the painting should be moved, moved to an empty, unused eye-level niche in the cathedral's north transept. There, before a table set with candles, pilgrims lined up to pay homage. Facing the *Man of Sorrows* was a sculpture of a black Madonna and Child, perched on a pedestal. The next day, December 21, 1994, newspapers across South Africa pealed the event. "Tutu's Yes to AIDS Painting" read the article's caption in Durban's *The Daily News*, the city's largest daily newspaper.

Hayden Proud, curator of painting and sculpture, South African National Gallery, Cape Town, wrote the following editorial. In large bold-face caption, it bore the title: "Christ with AIDS Painting Justified and in Line with Artistic Precedent."

An image of Jesus Christ suffering from AIDS painting by visiting artist Maxwell Lawton has generated commentary in your column that is largely mindless, uninformed, biased and ahistorical.

Mr. Lawton has provided local amateur theologians and self-appointed "art experts" with much to think about concerning the interface of AIDS and Christianity. It is a pity that the level of debate in this city should be so low, ranging from death threats made against the artist and openly declared intentions to destroy the canvas to the sanctimonious cant that has appeared in the Press. So much for the ideal of tolerance in the new South Africa. Isaiah prophesied Christ's suffering as follows…"the crowds were appalled on seeing him – so disfigured did he look – that he seemed no longer human…without beauty, no looks to attract our eyes, a being despised and rejected by men, a man of sorrows and familiar with suffering, a man to make people screen their faces; he was despised and we took no account of him…we thought of him as someone punished, struck by God and brought low…they gave him a grave with the wicked…but on him lies a punishment that brings us peace, and through his wounds we are healed." (Isaiah 52:13 – 53:12)

During the Black Death of the 1300s in Germany, wooden "plague" crucifixes were carved which accentuated and emphasized Christ's horrifying suffering in terms of his human incarnation and his human flesh. In 1510, at Isenheim, the Anthonite order of hospital monks, which was solely devoted to the physical and spiritual care of those dying from an infectious gangrenous disorder, commissioned an altarpiece for their church from the painter Matthias Grünewald (1460–1528).

Its central subject was the Crucifixion. Grünewald rendered the body of Christ with harrowing attention to detail and added to it the same symptoms of disease, the lesions of Christ's suffering humanity on earth. This altarpiece [is] one of the greatest achievements of late medieval art. It is an eloquent theological exposition on the mortality of Christ's human flesh and, in another panel, of its transfigured resurrection from the grave.

Today the mystical Body of Christ, his Church, is similarly affected by a new scourge, a new incurable infection and a new fear. This is HIV infection and AIDS. If a single member of Christ's mystical body – a single Christian – is infected it affects the whole, for all are vulnerable and all are members of this body. Implicit, therefore, is the notion of Christ's body having AIDS.

Mr. Lawton's concept of Christ with AIDS is not only in line with artistic precedent, but can be justified in terms of the metaphorical references to Christ's Body which abound in Scripture.

Ultimately, this is a story of courage – of conviction. Those who can follow a principle of truth will stand in the face of others unwaveringly. Allowing that principle of truth to prevail will, ultimately, bring about transformation in community.

Note: The italicized paragraph above was written by Catherine Kapikian specifically for this reprint.

About the author

Catherine Kapikian is founder and director of the pioneering Henry Luce III Center for the Arts and Religion at Wesley Theological Seminary in Washington, DC. She is a member of the faculty in the interdisciplinary field of art and theology. An acclaimed artist, her work, inclusive of paraments, vestments, banners, tapestries, and fiber with wood installations, can be seen in a variety of worship spaces in every major Christian denomination, as well as interfaith military chapels, and synagogues. Many of her large format works, like needlepoint tapestries behind altars, are designed by her and fabricated by members of the community in what she calls "participatory aesthetics." In this manner, the installation becomes the work of the people. In addition to teaching, giving workshops, and supervising resident artists at the Center, she writes and publishes articles in the field of art and theology.

PART 3

Transforming Biblical and Theological Understandings

Increasingly I was coming to see that theology, like religion itself, was really an art form. In every tradition, I was discovering, people turned to art when they tried to express or evoke a religious experience: to painting, music, architecture, dance or poetry. They rarely attempted to define their apprehension of the divine in logical discourse or in the scientific language of hard fact. Like all art, theology is an attempt to express the inexpressible. As T.S. Eliot said of poetry, it is a "raid on the inarticulate."
– KAREN ARMSTRONG, THE SPIRAL STAIRCASE: MY CLIMB OUT OF DARKNESS

The Language of Light

Keri K. Wehlander

In ancient times, people would erect stelae to help them find their way, or to mark significant events. These were often made from stone, and had inscriptions carved into them. Markers of this kind that remain today serve as sources of significant information about the stories and beliefs of cultures that have preceded our own.

When artist Sarah Hall reflects on her *Lux Nova* project, she thinks of it in much the same way. "It is a contemporary stela – it has a deep resonance with the wayfinding stelae from ancient times."

Lux Nova is an extraordinary stained glass installation located on the campus of Regent College in Vancouver, British Columbia. It is the central element in a 40-foot-high glass tower that rises above Regent's underground theological library. At first glance, the viewer is drawn in by the aesthetics of the design and the interesting architecture. But there are many intricate layers to this project, each revealing something about the ongoing process of theological reflection in a contemporary setting.

The tower itself is called the *True North Wind Tower*. Designed by architects Clive Grout and Walter Francl, it provides natural ventilation for the library below, thereby reducing the need to rely on electricity. The mechanical system of the library is based on the concept of a radiant heating and cooling system, and the triangular tower plays a key role in this green technology. Regent was intentional in making these choices as a part of their theological understanding that we are meant to be caretakers of God's creation.

There is another significant element to the design of the wind tower. The tower points up at an angle, and is directed at the North Star. As Dal Schindell, Director of Publications at Regent College, reflects, "We are located at the main gate to the University of British Columbia, and the tower is the most visible public art project for both campuses. It communicates our concern for the world and our encouragement to others to shine your light wherever you are. The tower directs us to the North Star – the one still point in our part of the universe. Ultimately, it is a reminder that humans need to be pointed to something that is true and is bigger than all of us."

Lux Nova participates in this layering of meaning in a way that makes it a North Star in its own right. It is the first photovoltaic art glass installation in North America. Photovoltaic modules collect solar energy, which can then be utilized for other energy needs. It is a green technology already used extensively in Europe, but relatively new to North America. Solar cells transform the glass facade into a clean, long-lasting energy source that does not emit harmful greenhouse gases. In this installation, the solar energy collected during the day is used at night to illuminate the stained glass and surrounding park with a changing LED light display.

Through this installation, Sarah Hall has explored an unexpected intersection: the ancient art of stained glass with the latest solar technology. In doing so, *Lux Nova* will provide a remarkable model for future design possibilities. Ursula Franklin, a renowned physicist and recipient of the Order of Canada, has high praise for Hall and *Lux Nova*:

> Sarah Hall [has] opened herself willingly to a further and unique extension of her craft: the inclusion of photovoltaic cells in her windows' overall design and purpose. She was willing to learn and experiment, moving into quite uncharted terrain…[She] is, to the best of my knowledge, the only Canadian artist who has taken this step of active collaboration with electronic engineers. The first public result of this collaboration – her windows at Regent College on the campus of the University of British Columbia – will, I am sure, be regarded in future as a seminal installation, showing how in the hands of a masterful artisan the craft can incorporate the oldest and the newest knowledge in one beautiful and functional work.

Remarkably, the photovoltaic glass is only the first layer in this innovative work. Hall describes the layers of glass as being "like pages in a book." The second layer of *Lux Nova* is made up of a series of twelve crosses that pattern the glass from bottom to top. Hall intentionally used a Greek cross, so that the general public encountering it would not immediately think in stereotypical terms about Christianity. Similarly, she hopes that the number twelve will open itself up for interpretation: the twelve disciples, the twelve tasks of Hercules, the twelve tribes of Israel, the twelve months in a year, and so on. The coloured crosses embedded in this layer of glass are made from dichroic glass, which is most commonly used for windshields on spacecraft!

The third layer of the work led Hall to do some interesting – and memorable – research. The theological setting and heavenward orientation of the tower made Hall think of the Lord's Prayer. As she thought about the beauty of the prayer, and its universal qualities, she decided to integrate it into the design. However, she wanted to incorporate it in Aramaic, since that was the language it was first spoken in. She contacted friend David Goa, Director of the Chester Ronning Centre at the University of Alberta, to ask for his assistance in finding a manuscript containing the text. He suggested that she contact a Chaldean church. The Chaldean church is one of the historic Christian communities of the Middle East that has preserved the use of the Aramaic language in their communities and their worship. She was able to locate a congregation in Toronto, and set up a meeting with Hanna Zora, the Chaldean Archbishop who serves there. At one point during their conversation, he sang the Lord's Prayer for her in Aramaic. Hall describes the moment as "beautiful" – one that will stay with her for a very long time. The Archbishop then transcribed the text for her, which became the source she used to etch the letters into the glass.

The final layer in the piece is a waterfall of coloured light, flowing in blues, violets and whites. Hall found that these colours particularly suited the West Coast environment. "The light is really different in Vancouver," she says, describing it as a "silvery kind of light." The waterfall also honoured patron Heather Alloway and her work with the organization "Living Water."

Part of the work on this layer involved designing the changing colours of the nighttime LED light display. Hall often works on her artwork with music playing in the background, and she credits the music of Canadian violinist Oliver Schroer as the source of inspiration for the gracefully moving coloured light display that she created.

Hall's fascination with the play and movement of light is a longstanding one. Michael Mills, a visual artist and Lutheran pastor who knows Hall, reflects on her work through the retelling of a story:

Sarah once told me a story about when she was a young girl and her father was chairing the building committee of their church. For a year, Sarah would accompany her father as the building committee toured churches every Sunday afternoon. At these times, Sarah would sit in the worship space with its coloured glass windows, and she would watch the gently changing patterns that the sun projected onto the walls as it traced its voyage across the heavens. It was then that she fell in love with the weight and movement and feel of light. As I see her work today, I see her still playing with the glory of simple sunlight as if she were a child. There is a richness and joy in her work that is deeper than words. It is the joy of the ephemeral, the joy of the spirit world which fills all space and all matter, if you have eyes to see. Sarah has eyes to see. And to experience her work is to return to a deep, unspoken part of one's self. It is to connect again with the holy.

Hall's affinity with light and colour led her to decide to study the art of creating stained glass. She enrolled in the Architectural Glass Program at Swansea College of Arts in Wales, and graduated with her Diploma in Architectural Glass from the City and Guilds of London Institute. After apprenticing with glass master Lawrence Lee, Hall spent a year in Jerusalem studying gold-leaf and techniques from the Middle East. She opened her own studio in Toronto in 1980, and as her projects increased in size, initiated a working relationship with a fabrication studio in Germany. Germany plays a leading role in European stained glass, as it has a well-established set of studios with highly trained artisans dedicated to its production. It was during one of Hall's visits to Germany that she first encountered the use of photovoltaic light and began to investigate the possibilities for using it in her own work.

She has created close to 1,000 stained glass art installations for sanctuaries, embassies and public spaces across North America, and has won numerous awards for these works. For Hall, every setting "has a language of its own." She examines every building carefully – along with its interplay with light – to understand how her work will interact with the space. When working in a church or synagogue, Hall does not ask what kind of colours or pictures they want. Instead, she asks them to describe their spirituality. In listening to the stories that this question generates, Hall always discovers a hidden "gem" that, along with the architecture, gives her a place to start from. In turn, her clients are likely to refer to the process of working with Hall – and the finished stained glass installation – as having a deep spiritual significance.

Sarah Hall's own spirituality lies at the core of her approach to her artistic work. As a Quaker, she notes, "We don't have a set creed. Faith is not something which is frozen in history, nor is it a fixed set of beliefs. It is something able to change and transform." Hall enters into her artistic projects with the same sensibility: "I don't have a set style that I bring to every project. I like to challenge myself by working on projects where I explore new techniques. My work continues to be a creative act, because I continue to learn more with every step." As for the underlying theology in her work, she says, "The power of stained glass comes from the colour and the movement of light itself. It can transform a space into something new. But if the picture that the stained glass forms is too literal, it can overtake this quality. This applies to faith as well. If it is static, it loses its primary power. We must be able to keep growing in our faith."

It is interesting to note that there is a strong language of light that is central to the Quaker tradition. To pray for someone is to "hold them in the light." George Fox, the founder of the Quakers, referred to the Holy Spirit as an "infinite ocean of light and love." The concept of "Inner Light" is one which Quakers use to refer to the presence of God within a person. No doubt, Hall's fascination with light has also been informed by these elements of Quaker spirituality.

As an artist, Hall cites the beauty of nature, scripture, her family and friends, art, music, and theatre as essentials for feeding her soul. She also relies on the "support and creativity" of her fabrication studio in Germany. She says, "They always lift my spirits." However, given the fact that there are 65 other artisans working in these facilities in Germany, she doesn't do her design work there. She has a solitary workspace in Toronto that she describes as being "something like a cloister." The space has large windows which are made of white glass. The colour in the glass begins with opaque white and moves through gradations until it becomes transparent. She says that the windows give this space a serene feeling that she finds conducive for her work.

She describes the work on *Lux Nova* as being very demanding from a technological point of view: "It's not as if there were a tremendous number of examples to draw upon. It was a steep learning curve for everyone. When I finally saw the light being collected from the sun, it felt great. I knew that it demonstrated that we don't have to depend on, exploit, or invade countries where oil and gas are found for our energy." Her hope is that this project will help to bring about change. "When people see an alternative energy source, they don't necessarily get excited. But when beauty and technology come together, it has the potential to inspire, and bring about wonderful possibilities."

The marriage of beauty and technology. A tower with layers of meaning. An installation that is the first of its kind. A place where theology, technology, ecology, and creativity meet. Sarah Hall is a deeply spiritual visionary who brings all these elements together through her own willingness to let the light inform, inspire, and transform her. She is fluent in the language of light. As a stela for our own time, there is no doubt that *Lux Nova* will shine a light to help us all find our way forward.

Sarah Hall is one of North America's best known stained glass artists. Her work has received numerous awards for outstanding liturgical art. Sara Hall's work can be viewed at <u>www.sarahhallstudio.com</u>.

About the author

Keri K. Wehlander (<u>www.creativeworship.ca</u>) is an author, hymn lyricist, and retreat leader. She is the series editor for *Experience! Faith Formation Curriculum for Adults* (Wood Lake Publishing Inc.) and the author of *Circles of Grace: Worship and Prayer in the Everyday* (United Church Publishing House). Her writings have been included in various anthologies in both North America and Europe. Keri is the editor of *Creating Change: The Arts as Catalyst for Spiritual Transformation*.

The Sower

Charles McCollough

For many years, I sculpted whenever I could, since I was on the national staff of the United Church of Christ. When I left that job in 2000, I finally had the opportunity to sculpt full-time.

Having studied theology, the subjects of my sculptures were often from the Bible. My first series of sculptures was based on the non-violent tactics of Jesus. I followed that with another series based on the Magnificat, and then another based on the Beatitudes. Most recently, I did a series on the parables. By working with a series, I could stay focused over many months on one theme. It also allowed me to dig deeply under the surface to see the political/economic context hidden in the text, and research available scholarly studies.

I use sculptured images to reach back to biblical texts because I believe that what doesn't get through to us in words may get through to us in images; some things in our lives are "too deep for words," but not necessarily for images. Thus, the text and images combined may go where words alone cannot go.

My four-year journey in sculpting the parables convinced me that the wisdom they contain is still rich and critically valuable for those of us who seek the way of Jesus. Just as Mark, Matthew, Luke, and Thomas applied the parables of Jesus to the needs of their day, we can apply them to the needs of our time.

The first step in my journey with the parables was to learn from the relevant scholarship about the context (economic, social, and political) in which they came to be, and to see if Jesus used the parables to speak in that context. Granted, this required imagination, with all the risks and the creative possibilities such imaginative interpretations present. I concluded that the parables, as well as Jesus' whole life and death make no sense if we don't account for the poverty of his peasant community life, and for the political oppression of the Roman occupation. Jesus' preaching and actions sought to heal both the physical and spiritual effects of that domination by an alien empire. This conclusion opens the parables so that they speak to the issues of poverty and oppression in all times – especially our own.

The second step was the creation of the sculptural images. This allowed me to move beyond a verbal, discursive, and conceptual understanding of the parables, to an imaginative, intuitive and visual one.

"The Sower" is based on Mark 4:1–23. My image is unusual in two ways. The Sower is a woman because women often do the farming in impoverished lands. And she is very proud, communicating in her features and posture the message that she will not be beaten down by the oppression of Rome and the patriarchy of that period. I think Jesus taught revolutionary non-violence by giving hope to the peasants. He showed them that they were worthy and blessed by God and could resist the domination of the empire of Rome and become part of the Empire of God. "The Sower" is doing that by becoming self-affirming as well as self-sufficient with her crop. Just as Jesus lifted her spirit, my spirit was lifted in the shaping of this piece. My hope is that she will do the same for others.

About the author

Charles McCollough worked for the national staff of the United Church of Christ in the areas of adult education and social justice after he completed his Ph.D. in theology. During the time he worked at the national office, he pursued his love of art, studying sculpture at the Pennsylvania Academy of Fine Arts, Johnson Atelier, the Princeton Art Association, and Mercer College. He has taught art and social ethics, sculpted, and lectured on themes such as human rights, peace and justice. He is the author of *The Art of Parables*; *Morality of Power*; *Heads of Heaven/Feet of Clay*; *Lifestyles of Faithfulness*; *To Love the Earth*; *Resolving Conflict with Justice*; and *Peace, and Faith Made Visible*.

Bible Study and Movement for Human Transformation

Walter Wink

It was 1954, and I was only nineteen when I first discovered that there is a somatic approach to Scripture. I was in a spiritual crisis and had found my way, providentially, to Camp Farthest Out, a pious but profound retreat program focusing on prayer. At one point, they put on Beethoven's *Moonlight Sonata* and asked us to express ourselves with pastels. Grabbing a large chunk of charcoal, I drew a scene more appropriate to *Night on Bald Mountain*. Looking at my creation, I suddenly realized that I was a wreck.

Later they put on a musical rendition of the Lord's Prayer and asked us to express the prayer with our bodies. I was tall, skinny, awkward, and embarrassed, but I got to my feet and tried to move. My mind said "Move!" but my body, like Balaam's ass, balked. I ordered it. It sneered. It was in that moment that I discovered that, notwithstanding my intellectual belief in God, my body was an atheist.

My body taught me two things. My hand somehow knew what my conscious mind had no inkling of: that I was in the thick of a spiritual crisis that would result in a profound reorganization of my life. My body also knew that my mind's rational deliberations about God had in no sense become incarnate. I was split, head and body, spirituality and sexuality, and reason and emotions. An ecstatic experience of God soon after not only did nothing to heal that split but also widened it. Now at least I knew I had a problem, and I knew what it was. I have spent my life since then trying to resolve it.

Why did my body have access to a wisdom of which my conscious mind knew nothing? How was it that Jesus' prayer, which I had been praying all my life, had not penetrated below my neck, as it were? I had been reading the Gospels devotionally for a long time; I had heard them weekly in church. What was so different about trying (and failing!) to "read" them with my flesh? I had always regarded my body as a slave and had subjected it to strict disciplines. Now it was staging a slave revolt, and nothing in my experience prepared me for it...

It was not until 1971, however, that I found a method that actually took these concerns about body-mind-spirit integration seriously and made them operational. I attended a seminar titled "The Records of the Life of Jesus" with the Guild for Psychological Studies at Four Springs in Middletown, California. Here, I found the Bible being studied by means of Socratic dialogue and a rich variety of exercises and experiments that sought to embody or incarnate the insights of Scripture into one's life. We studied the baptism of Jesus, and then we did a picture of it. We mimed all the characters in the parable of the Prodigal Son. We walked wooded mountain trails reciting mantras drawn from the Lord's Prayer. We surrounded Bible study with hours of meditative silence. We tried to locate our own inner paralytics by fashioning them with clay. I found this strange, exhilarating, and immensely profitable, as one part of my being after another responded, as if found for the first time by means of these imaginative exercises.

However, that was not all. We did play readings, we moved spontaneously to music, we meditated before selected pieces of art, we danced, we built altars and fashioned impromptu rituals, we mimed poetry, we studied the stars, we practiced contemplation, and we reflected on myths from the world's religions, especially Native American. It was a rich spread centered on incarnating in our own bodies the life of God incarnated by Jesus. We were, in effect, asking ourselves what would happen if we stopped thinking of Jesus as the sole incarnation of God and saw him rather as the guide who showed us how to incarnate God ourselves.

I had always wanted to dance freely and with abandon. I had even taken a class in jazz dancing in college (I was the only male in the class; my fraternity brothers, who worked off their physical education requirement by playing Ping-Pong, watched me, leering and laughing, from the balcony); not surprisingly, that did not take. I had been attending movement classes for several years, but I still regarded it as an athletic challenge, a matter of making my body do what I told it. Though I was a fairly good athlete, I was still awkward and basically afraid that if I started cavorting around, I would simply fall on my face.

One afternoon, during that first seminar at Four Springs, the leaders put on Sibelius' *The Oceanides* and invited us to move to it in the swimming pool. This was a major breakthrough for me. No matter what I did – if I lost my balance – the water would catch me. I could simply continue the movement under water. More important yet, the music somehow seemed to know my own heart perfectly. It was as if the music was no longer coming into me from outside, but from my own depths; it was as if the music were being played by my own heart. After it was over, I lay by the pool, astonished that someone from a different country and a different time could know so precisely the innermost feelings of my heart. For the first time, I had a clear sense that we are not isolated monads discretely separated from one another, but that we are actually linked together by mysterious connections I scarcely understood but could no longer deny.

Clearly, all of this could have been done without the Bible as the focus of our task. Later, I attended other seminars at Four Springs with different themes: the ring trilogies of Tolkien and Wagner, the Iroquois myth of the Secret of No-Face, the Navaho myth of Changing Woman. However, none was as powerful for me as the encounter with Scripture. The process of freeing my body up had taken place in the context of the symbol system in which I found my meaning and identity. In some ways, the prohibitions that had led to my personal and physical rigidities appeared to come from the Bible, and it was essential that the transformations I was experiencing were not only "licensed" by Scripture but also provoked by it. The Bible was giving me new insights about my body, my being, and my destiny, and I was gaining a new way of regarding the Bible.

When I returned to teach New Testament at Union Theological Seminary in New York the next fall, I began to incorporate the more holistic approach I had learned from the Guild for Psychological Studies. In the first session of a class on the Gospel of Mark, I had the students do a picture of the baptism of Jesus without consulting any commentaries, just as we had done at Four Springs. Only this was taking place in an academic setting, and I was under pressure to do rigorous graduate-level teaching. As a doctoral student, I had done an exhaustive exegesis of Jesus' baptism, so I was pretty sure I was on top of the literature. I wanted to see if drawing the picture might provide an alternative route to knowledge, or a different way of knowing. In their pictures, the students collectively scored every significant exegetical point it had taken me four months in the library to discover! It was not my intention to substitute art for exegesis; but the point had been made. There is more than one avenue to exegetical insight. "The heart has its reason the mind knows not of" (Pascal). How much richer the return if we would use both together!...

The students, for their part, loved it; for once, their whole beings were being engaged in an encounter with Scripture, with reality and with God. Powerful things were happening to them as a result of encountering Scripture. We built a weekend retreat into the course, with time for movement and silence. Teaching became midwifery in the transformation of those who felt called to become enablers of transformation. They were learning, not only a content, but a method – one that they could use in many different contexts (churches, prisons, retirement homes, social change struggles, and nontraditional ministries).

One of my biggest complaints with theological education is that teaching through the lecture mode, while sometimes necessary and even effective, is almost totally untransferable to a parish setting. Except in very few churches where the membership is heavily laced with holders of graduate degrees, lectures are ineffective and usually unwanted in the parish setting. Here was a method, however, that could serve as the medium for graduate education and, at the same, be learned in the process of imbibing information. It could be used in virtually any conceivable small group setting, and some not so small. The professor, rather than modeling a methodology largely irrelevant to the needs of Christian workers (except future seminary teachers – and not even these, if they were to use this method), would be modeling an approach immediately transferable to other situations.

It all made so much sense to me. However, it was apparently unsettling when laughter emanated from my classes as students presented Jesus' resurrection appearance in John 21 as a farce (including Peter's dressing to spring into the water and the disciples counting all 153 of the fish). The use of oil pastels in a graduate seminary seemed puerile, and the shouting of the Lord's Prayer at the top of our lungs to get a physiological sense of the importance and meaning of the imperative construction of each of its petitions was understandably disturbing. Besides, there was a fiscal crisis. Therefore, it was not really surprising, though still painful, when I was denied tenure...

Through the good offices of Professor Robert Lynn, who was then doubling up at Union Seminary and as the head of Auburn Seminary, I began to work at Auburn doing continuing education.

Auburn fully supported my approach. Perhaps I should explain that Auburn had been a Presbyterian seminary in Auburn, New York, until it closed in 1939 and moved down to Union Seminary, where it continued a shadow existence, funding endowed chairs at Union, providing scholarships for Presbyterian students, and operating a summer program for clergy. Under Bob Lynn's leadership, Auburn launched a full-scale continuing education program for clergy and laity. It has no academic classes, offers no degrees, and has no student body. In practical terms, this means that I spend a great deal of time on the road, doing workshops and retreats all over the United States and Canada.

Something was still missing, however. Though I was doing many exercises that involved art, mime, and role playing, I was not using movement or music – and that had been one of the most decisively important elements in my own transformation. I had taken many movement classes, but quite honestly felt no vocation for leading movement – and no clear idea how to do so. However, my wife, June Keener-Wink, had also taken these movement classes, had been in a movement leadership group, and had been teaching movement to children for almost a decade. What we lacked was a model for interpreting Bible study with body movement. With great trepidation, we experimented by leading a few weekend retreats together. People responded affirmatively even though we were largely unable to explain how Scripture and movement integrate. It was clear that the participants were doing the integration themselves. We have been trying ever since to make connections between Scripture, movement, and life. I wish I could tell you that we have, after eight years of working together, completed that task, but we are far from doing so. As I reflect on it now, I am not even sure it is necessary to make this connection consciously.

There is no intrinsic connection between body work and Scripture. They can each be profitably done separately. What we have discovered, however, is that when we work alone, the results are greatly diminished. There is something that happens when the central symbol system of the Christian faith is experienced both intellectually and organismically.

Perhaps I should try to give you some idea of what June does in the body movement session. To introduce the movement session she sometimes makes a statement like this:

> The body of Christ is made up of bodies. We cannot be a part of
> the body of Christ except in our bodies. The notion of the "body
> of Christ" was Paul's way of naming the new reality that had

come about in the events triggered by Jesus. The early church had experienced a new mutation in human evolution. Human evolution, as scientists have pointed out, is no longer physical but social. The new human possibility emerging, which Paul called the "new creation," is a corporate reality in which the individual is not swallowed up by the collective, but each person is on a journey to authentic being-in-community. This new experience involved neither the tyranny of the group over the individual, nor the rugged individualism that rejects all group relationship or accountability. It represents a new potential, possible only after people have fought free of the dominance of the group and have found their own path through responding to the guidance of God.

This new corporate body is made up of bodies. And our freedom to relate to one another and to respond to the promptings of the Holy Spirit depends on the way we relate to our own bodies. Our availability to God is to a great extent determined by how free we are spontaneously to respond to what God presents to us as bodies.

Historically, the church has denied the body and has split body from soul, nurturing only the soul and repressing, ignoring, or disciplining the body. Such an attitude is unbiblical. There are no separate words for "soul" or "body" in Hebrew. There is, rather, one word that combines them both – *nephesh*, "animated body, living being." The Hebrews simply could not regard the human person as split into separate parts, but as an integral being. This view is now being affirmed by modern medicine.

We do movement therefore as a way of integrating physical and spiritual, outer and inner, and the substance of our flesh and the substance of faith. The movement is explicitly an attempt to heal the ancient split that fractures our beings and sets us at odds with our bodies. Our goal is to recover a sense of our bodies as temples of the Holy Spirit within us.

As with any art, one cannot always make direct correlations between the movement and Bible study. But we trust from experience that these correlations are being made nonetheless at the core of the self. Bible study cannot be holistic if it deals only with the intellect. Only when the whole person is involved with Scripture can we hope to heal the split between body and spirit and enable people to become more authentic human beings-in-community...

As we have worked with people in groups, we have discovered that their capacity to recover the freedom to move is associated with a new self-image. They discover self-acceptance despite not being perfect according to the cultural norms of beauty. The ability to respond spontaneously in one's body means that a person is overcoming inhibitions and terrors often dating back to childhood. What is being enacted is precisely the healing that Scripture itself describes. When we become capable of organismic spontaneity – that is, when we are able to respond appropriately to the everlasting goodness of life in the moment – we find that we are living in the presence of God. We are more supple, more vulnerable, and freed from frozen bodies incapable of dancing to the occasion. We are available to God in a new way, more attentive to what the Spirit wants done, and more willing to do it, even if it requires doing something with our bodies that would previously have embarrassed us and thus prevented our response.

The movement is not a tool for deepening our understanding of Scripture; it is a way of bringing about in our bodies the new possibilities for living that the gospel proclaims have now, in Jesus, broken into the world. We are not trying simply to grasp what the Bible means but to become the people that the Bible proclaims. We are not just learning about the Bible but attempting to incarnate the God revealed by Jesus, who incarnated that God. We are not merely examining the doctrine of the Holy Spirit but opening our bodies, quite literally, to become the temples of the Holy Spirit within us.

About the author

Dr. Walter Wink (www.walterwink.com) is Professor Emeritus of Biblical Interpretation at Auburn Theological Seminary in New York City. Previously, he was a parish minister and taught at Union Theological Seminary in New York City. In 1989–1990 he was a Peace Fellow at the United States Institute of Peace. In 2006, Walter and June Wink were recipients of the Martin Luther King, Jr. Peace Prize from the Fellowship of Reconciliation for their renowned work as teachers of nonviolent theory and practice across the world.

Humor and Grace

Keri K. Wehlander

Imagine creating a day retreat for yourself. You pack a picnic, pull on your hiking boots, and ask one of your longtime friends to go with you. Then you spend the day wandering forest paths while taking turns storytelling your way through the Bible. This is precisely what Dan Erlander did with Charles Mays on a bright summer day in Washington's Cascade Mountains. The stories sprang to life for both of them that day – and they discovered that the humor had a chance to emerge.

This day of storytelling marked the beginning for Erlander's book *Manna and Mercy*, which blends a passion for justice with sophisticated biblical scholarship into a remarkable book of simple drawings, hand-lettered pages, and gentle humor. The book is 93 pages in length, but took seven years to create. It was definitely a labor of love.

One of his favorite drawings in the book is the one he did representing the Last Supper, because he had the opportunity to show that women were included around the table.

Another favorite drawing represents the return of the prodigal son. The father is holding his younger son, while the older son is grumbling in the background.

It is clear to anyone who comes into contact with Dan Erlander that humor is a key element of his faith. "The Bible is filled with humor, and we miss most of it. Think of all those people out there who think that Christians are all crabby. And what we really are supposed to be about is grace. Humor is deeply connected with grace. We need the truthfulness of laughter to understand the inconsistencies of human power. We need laughter to recognize the absurdity of the world and to be able to delight in the world around us. Laughter takes us off guard, so that the living word can reach us."

He attributes his sense of humor to his mother in particular. "She made people laugh all the time. She was a bit of a stand-up comedian." Consequently, his family loved to laugh together.

Drawing was something that Erlander did from an early age. He drew all through school – and on one of his report cards, his teacher added this reprimand: "Daniel must understand that math class is not art class!"

He majored in art in college, but continually felt a pull to attend seminary. He wasn't sure how to choose between what felt like two separate callings. One day, he went to one of his religion professors to talk through his dilemma. Erlander marks this conversation as a turning point for him.

The professor, Kenneth Christopherson, said, "Go to seminary. You will find a way to put your two callings together."

While in seminary, Erlander discovered that cartoons were a great way to make a point. With his trademark humor, he would draw cartoons that poked fun at whatever they were studying, and pass them around the class.

Once he was ordained and working in a congregation, he discovered an interest in photography. He began to create "slide sermons" – meditations for worship that were made up of his photo images set to music.

In 1979, Erlander was invited to spend a year in Washington, serving as pastor of Holden Village, an ecumenical retreat center rooted in the Lutheran tradition. It was here that he discovered that he could convert complex theological and biblical concepts into simple drawings and accessible language. His first handwritten, illustrated book, *Baptized We Live*, was begun at this time. His idea was to create a teaching tool to help readers understand what it meant to be a "Lutheran" Christian.

One of the concepts he speaks about in the book is the "living word," a term he frequently uses in conversation. In the book, he writes, "What is the Living Word? First we need to understand the opposite of 'Living Word,' which is 'Dead Word' – truth packaged in propositions with which we can argue, agree or disagree. In contrast, Living Word is truth manifest in an event, a story or an encounter through which God addresses us and calls for repentance, revolution, a redirection of life. The New Testament word for this change is *metanoia*, which means 'to turn around and go in the opposite direction.'"

Erlander finished the book once he had returned to the congregation he was serving. He self-published it, and had 1,000 copies printed. Within six months, he was sold out. From the responses he received, he realized that this method of teaching by pictures and words was truly touching people. His professor's prediction had come true: Erlander had found a way to live out his double calling as pastor and artist.

Since publishing *Baptized We Live*, Erlander has gone on to write and illustrate a book that assists parents and sponsors in understanding baptism; a companion book which assists youth and adults being baptized in understanding baptism; a game "board" which describes the Christian journey from a Lutheran perspective; *Manna and Mercy: A Brief History of God's Unfolding Promise to Mend the Entire Universe*; and *A Place for You* – a first-communion book for children complete with an invitation to find pictures of "the crabby people" who were upset with Jesus in a drawing of the feeding of the five thousand.

Given their accessibility, his books have become resources all over the world. They have been translated into Chinese, Spanish, Portuguese, Latvian, Vietnamese, Japanese, and Russian.

There have been many powerful responses to these books. Recently, a man came up to him and told him that the reason that he had chosen Christianity as his spiritual path was because of one of the books Erlander had written.

Ultimately, Erlander feels that his drawings have a way of working around the defenses that people put up. "When you counter a person with a logical argument, there is an inner trap door that stays shut. But if you tell them a story, and use humor, that trap door opens – it gets through defenses and self-righteousness, and, as a result, the living word has a chance to get through."

Erlander finds that his work even has a transformative effect on him. "It keeps converting me. Whenever I get crabby, these pictures have a way of bringing me back to the utter simplicity of the Gospel. It is so clear. I can laugh at myself again."

His unique style of writing and illustration often takes his readers by surprise. A woman named Judith left these comments in her review of *Baptized We Live* on Amazon.com: "Wow! This book is sooo uplifting, happy, refreshingly un-churchy. If you can picture Charles Shultz's Snoopy reincarnated as a Lutheran minister and writing about what he believes in... you're getting close to what this book is like... Erlander has hand printed, and hand illustrated...the entire book. He apparently writes like this all the time (he summarized the whole Bible this way and called it "Manna and Mercy"...) Who but the reincarnation of Snoopy would take on the whole Bible with one pencil and a ream of blank paper?... Words alone don't give a true idea of the book...the reader has to open the covers and join in the multi-media experience created from one pencil and one gentle mind that obviously has spent time laughing first-hand with God."

Artist and pastor, humorist and scholar, gentle reformer, Dan Erlander seeks to create a joyous response to a God who is continually surprising us. And, ultimately, these surprises have the capacity for transformation. As he observes, "Art that surprises or throws us off balance is often the greatest art, because we have to make a decision to walk away or be drawn into it and be changed."

With Erlander's help, we just might make the choice of being changed – laughing all the while.

About the author

Keri K. Wehlander (www.creativeworship.ca) is an author, hymn lyricist, and retreat leader. She is the series editor for *Experience! Faith Formation Curriculum for Adults* (Wood Lake Publishing Inc.) and the author of *Circles of Grace: Worship and Prayer in the Everyday* (United Church Publishing House). Her writings have been included in various anthologies in both North America and Europe. Keri is the editor of *Creating Change: The Arts as Catalyst for Spiritual Transformation*.

Jesus proclaimed that the new reality, the reign of God, is filled with blessed people who are poor, merciful, pure in heart, hungry, weeping, and persecuted. They are also PEACEMAKERS — people who understand that God's compassion has no limits. The "wombishness" of Yahweh embraces even the enemy. Divine love surprises the adversary with unconditional mercy. Everybody, absolutely everybody, is included in the embrace of God [LUKE 6:27-36].

Jesus had a name for those who follow God's way of enemy love. They are called sons and daughters of God which means IMITATORS of the divine life [LUKE 6:35].

Knowing compassion to be Yahweh's deepest desire, Jesus believed that there is no time when mercy is inappropriate. This understanding got Jesus into deep trouble with the religious leaders because he did not stop healing the sick on the Sabbath day. Jesus continued to help people in need during this beautiful "gift of time" which God gave to the wilderness people. Those who secured their status by keeping all the rules called Jesus a Sabbath breaker. They called Jesus' loving actions "breaking the Sabbath." They were horrified, completely horrified. Their response was to...

MURMUR, MURMUR, MURMUR, MURMUR, MURMUR, MURMUR.

PART 4

Transforming Worship

Sung words affect me in ways that said words do not. Where sermons slide off, hymns sink in. Days later, I can be minding my own business, doing something as secular as sweeping the kitchen floor or balancing the checkbook, when I begin to hum a hymn tune. If I stop to identify it, I can usually recover the words, which are often so pertinent to my situation that they arrive like Priority Mail from God.

— Barbara Brown Taylor, Leaving Church: A Memoir of Faith

Moving Spirit

Lindsay McLaughlin

© Stan Barouh

The elderly woman in the seventh pew slowly, hesitantly, lifted her left arm. The gesture was tentative, but the expression on her face was intent. She was absorbed in the drama unfolding before her, that of the death of Lazarus and the desperate pleas from his sisters to his dear friend Jesus to come to his side.

It was Lent, and the church was making an extra effort to make the scripture readings meaningful and alive. In this instance, dancers were interpreting the words as they were read, using simple, clear movements that the congregation could "echo" (mirror, really) from their seats. Standing on the wide step before the altar, caught up in the synthesis of the gestures I was making and the anguish and fearsome joy of the story, I faced the people in the pews. It was evident that by using more than just their ears, those in the church that morning were accessing the story and its meaning at a deeper, inner level. I had only to glance at the woman in front of me to confirm this.

One can sometimes think of "liturgical dance" as a means by which professionals or well-trained amateurs enhance the worship experience using dance with religiously themed musical accompaniment. That understanding of the art form limits its profound possibilities for deepening the spiritual journey of anyone who can lift their hands and breathe. If "liturgy" means "the work of the people" then the people can do "liturgical" dance.

This was the vision of one of my inspirational mentors in the field and one whom I consider the founding mother of the dance-in-worship movement, Carla De Sola. As far back as the early 1970s, she had already been encouraging many congregations around the country to use movement in church. She opens her seminal handbook of dance, *The Spirit Moves*, with a prayer that captures her heart:

> I pray that everyone, sitting cramped inside a pew, body lifeless, spine sagging and suffering, weary with weight and deadness, will be given space in which to breathe and move, will be wooed to worship with beauty and stillness, song and dance – dance charged with life, dance that lifts up both body and spirit, and we will be a holy, dancing, loving, praying and praising people.

How and why can dance and movement "lift up both body and spirit" and enrich the worship life of a congregation? When we move our bodies in response to a thought, an image, a yearning, a joy, we inevitably shift from the verbal and defined to the realm of the spirit. We are externalizing, or expressing in our physical being, some internal impulse that is beyond words. Dance is this movement stylized, so it draws people into, as Carla says, these "mysteries,"

> ...through the use of basic, nonliteral materials. These include rhythms, dynamics, shapes, subtle and heightened creations of moods and feelings. I think of dance, and all the arts, as bridges between the visible and the invisible world of the spirit.

In more than 25 years as a dancer and participant in liturgical dance ministries I have been witness to this connection countless times. I have danced in the all-purpose rooms of recreation centers where small, independent congregations meet, in cathedrals and in the sanctuaries of many churches. I have used dance to interpret scripture as well as traditional hymns, contemporary gospel, modern church music, and even silence. Everywhere the experience is the same – both the dancers and the watchers have new dimensions of understanding open within them.

While I have participated in numerous liturgical dance groups, I have also danced in worship to mark the most sacred moments of my own life: my wedding (yes, *really*, during the *service*), at every one of the baptisms of my three sons, and at the funeral of a dear friend. This is because, for me, dance *is* prayer. It is truly the best way I know to express my sense of connection with the divine – a channel of grace. It *is* sacramental.

Dance particularly speaks to me because I am a trained dancer and have danced all my life. But the good news for churches and people of faith everywhere is that most of those I have danced with "liturgically" over the years have never set foot in a dance studio. The majority are open-minded people responding to an inner call to explore the mind-spirit-body connection who are willing to take a risk. Movement need not be elaborate to be effective. Given only a few simple pointers, people are able to express themselves in movements of profound beauty. All body types and abilities can dance. As another of my mentors, Kathryn Fredgren, once stated in a liturgical dance workshop, "Everyone can do a happy hop."

Recently, for example, during a "meditative arts" retreat on gratefulness attended by members of several churches, we led a simple circle dance expressing the sense of people on a journey, going forward in faith together. As we walked slowly in the circle, first one way, then the other, we sang, "we are going…heaven knows where we are going…we will get there…heaven knows how we will get there…we know we will…" As I looked around the circle, more than a few had moist, joyful eyes – just walking, one foot then the other, and singing.

I believe that we, the faith community of the wider church, will indeed "get there" and fulfill Carla's vision of a "dancing…praying people." I experience it on Sundays all the time – in my own heart, and on the faces of elderly women in the seventh pews of churches everywhere.

About the author

Lindsay McLaughlin is a dancer, writer and member of the resident staff of the Rolling Ridge Study Retreat near Harpers Ferry, West Virginia. She currently dances with St. Martin's Liturgical Dance Ministry and with Carla Perlo, founding director of Dance Place, in Washington, DC.

Doorway to the Sacred

Susan Short

The arts have always been part of my faith journey. I anticipate an encounter with sacred presence each time I experience the music of an organ or piano, the sight of a coloured window or the imagery of a painting, or the sweeping movements of a dancer.

I am a child of the United Church of Canada, with strong Methodist roots on my father's side, and Baptist on my mother's side. The church has always been a presence in my life. Even when we stayed at my grandparent's cottage in the summer, we would hold Sunday worship in the living room if we were unable to drive into town to attend the local church. Nana would choose the hymns and Grandpa would play the piano. We would sing at the top of our lungs from memory or from the old blue hymnbook. Someone, usually my dad, would read a story from the Bible and talk a bit about it. We were encouraged to chime in, discuss, and even draw pictures in response. We sat in comfortable overstuffed chairs in the presence of beautiful flower bouquets from the garden. From a very young age, I felt worship could be whatever you created together.

I grew up hearing about my great-grandfather who was a stained glass artist. As a young girl, I saw a beautiful window that he had created in a church in London, Ontario. I wondered, even then, how a person could have within themselves a source and inspiration to create a piece so spirit-filled that it would speak to all who entered the building. His eye for beauty was also expressed through the extensive flower gardens he created around his country home. This gift passed to his eldest daughter, my grandmother, who had a natural talent with flowers. She judged shows and taught flower arranging around the Toronto area and brought this gift to her church. Even in her later years, when she was unable to attend services, someone would come and pick up her flower arrangements to decorate the chancel. My mother carries this tradition on today, making bouquets from her beautiful gardens to lend beauty to the sanctuary of her church.

The idea of contributing my artistic gifts to my church came early to me and morphed into an understanding that all gifts are welcomed and needed. As a young teenager, I was encouraged to take my love of the piano into my Sunday school, where I played children's hymns for the small opening worship several years in a row.

As an adult, I have found ways of using my love of storytelling in the Sunday schools of various congregations I have belonged to. I always felt that taking part in a story is as much fun as hearing or watching it unfold. So, when I was asked to be part of a worship planning team one year, my contribution involved a six-week storytelling series based on the hymn, "Tell Me the Stories of Jesus." Each week, a different group of children came up to the chancel to act out one of the stories. It was powerful and it involved all ages.

It seems to me that the presence of creative arts in worship awakens our imaginations – it provides a doorway to the sacred. In fact, "Doorways to the Sacred" was the theme for a congregational retreat I took part in a few years ago. During the retreat, we created different experiences or "doorways" for people to reflect on and work with. My dear friend Monica, who is a visual artist, was inspired to paint several variations of sacred doorways, and witnessing those paintings was a high point for all of us.

Looking back, some of the most memorable worship experiences I have taken part in integrated some element of the arts in them. Interestingly enough, they have often been part of a journey through a liturgical season.

One Advent, the call to worship each week was done as an interpretive dance. I particularly remember one young woman moving up the aisle expressing the joys and confusions of Mary's pregnancy. It was such a powerful experience. I found that it made so much sense to have scripture interpreted in this way.

At our home congregation of Wilmot United in Fredericton, I had an experience that was truly astounding. Beautiful stained glass windows line both sides of this 150-year-old sanctuary. Six artists had been asked to choose a window and interpret it in their own medium. Each week during Lent, one new piece was hung close to the window it was interpreting. Then all the creations were combined with a final arched top piece, making seven "panes." On Easter morning, this greeted us as one huge window hanging at the front of the sanctuary. I had been down by the river for the sunrise service, and when we walked back into the darkened sanctuary, someone turned a spotlight on the newly formed "window." I stopped in my tracks. It was spellbinding – a perfect way to interpret a journey and a final rising that mere words can never describe properly.

During another Lent, my beloved husband Peter, a minister in the United Church of Canada, encouraged one of our congregations to turn the narthex into an art gallery. The idea was that entering the sanctuary through an artistic experience would help us slow down and pay attention. I have a profound memory of one of the pieces of art – the wing of a bird coming out from the wall at a right angle. The wing was grey, the colour of ashes, and included soft feathers. The artist had written some words to accompany the piece. When I first saw it, I was gripped in a moment of grief. The wing touched something very deep within me. Later in the service we learned a new hymn: "Dust and ashes touch our face… Holy Spirit come… Take us by the hand and lead us…through the desert sands/bring us living water."[1]

In a split second, the words, the tune, and that ash-coloured wing transported me into the desert with Jesus. I felt God's presence and deep sorrow for God's children the world over. Even to this day, I cannot fully sing that beautiful hymn – I hum and weep it instead.

As I search my memory, I realize that worship has always been a place of creative possibilities. Beauty, texture, form, movement, sound – as our own bodies use all of the senses to live and move in this world, so our worship of God should incorporate all of these. Worship feels grounded and rich when all the senses are involved.

Artists, musicians, and storytellers through the ages have interpreted the faith journey for us, using the gift of creativity. I am thankful for the wide expression of these gifts, as I think it is impossible for there to be only one way to come to God. As we each travel our path, there are many ways to describe God and to celebrate life and community. How could it be otherwise, when you see the astounding diversity of all living things? The possibilities are just as infinite for worship. All these gifts – music, art, movement, story – point to the Creator, to the mystery that is God, awakening the sacred within us all.

About the author

Susan Short is a teacher and adult educator with a passion for writing, gardening and photography. She happily participates in the life of her home congregation of Wilmot United Church and increasingly shares in leadership of spiritual retreats with her husband, Peter. Sue and Peter live near the banks of the Saint John River in Fredericton, New Brunswick with an unruly Golden Retriever (Rudy), and are the proud parents of four grown children and grandparents of two precious wee girls.

[1] FROM *DUST AND ASHES TOUCH OUR FACE* BY BRIAN WREN

Song and Story with All Ages

Linnea Good

"Utterly amazed, they asked: 'Are not all these people who are speaking grown-ups? Then how is it that each of us hears them in our own kid-language?'" (Acts, as the Children Tell It, Chapter 2)

© Greg Johnson

Is there anybody who would like to come up and sing a song with me?" I often get up from the piano, stand in the middle of the chancel, and ask this question. Although I never say, "Are there any *children*...?" it is almost always children who come up – running or shyly walking or crawling. I love it – this hilarious and disjunct moment when children ask themselves if they dare join me for the unknown and public what-next, while many grown-ups don't even know they have been invited.

Some would say most of the children come up because they are "natural performers." Some will say that younger children are less inhibited than those of us who live by the cruel codes of coolness. Some say kids are just glad to stop sitting. I say that mostly they come up because *the song is worth it*. Something that happened in the group as we sang together has filled them, and convinced them that – if it's been good down *here*, it's going to be better up *there*. Possibly a mountaintop experience.

And so it *does become* a mountaintop experience – one in which the Spirit's constant invitation is suddenly recognized, allowed, opened into. It's about trust.

Sophie shouts "Yahoo!" from her mother's arms in the balcony, right in the middle of worship. A baby calls out as the last note of the organ echoes out across the stone walls of the church. Isaac swings little arms across his body, legs arcing out into the aisle wildly, as drums and guitar lead him into dance. The song is worth it. The song will say it. The song will lead it.

Do I need to tell you that music fills our body with oxygen, fills our left and right brains with synaptic fireworks, fills our bodies with a sense of our connected wholeness? That singing is good for our health, for our self-esteem, for our relationship with our neighbour? The song is worth it.

I have this feeling that it was *this* that Jesus was talking about when he said that grown-ups needed to surrender into a childlike spirit to really live in God. It wasn't about innocence – whoever thought that children were innocent? For me, it is the willingness to enter into the moment, to trust that what is offered is worth it.

As a musician and storyteller, I can tell you that one of the things I love best about children is this gift of totally entering into an experience. Imagination takes them to a place that is almost liminal – a space between this world and the next. I have sometimes walked into the "thin place" that is the imaginary world of my child and have known that when their gaze crossed mine, it was not seeing me at all. Young children can become so caught up in the singing of a song that they don't even sing! I believe they *think* they are singing, but the world which they are inhabiting as they sing is interior. When asked, children will join in the telling, acting, moving and responding to a story immediately and completely.

One year, I led a group of seven- and eight-year-olds in church school for the whole season of Lent. Each week we progressively built a "desert" in our classroom. In the first week, we laid down a floor covering that became our desert sand; the next week we brought desert creatures and plants from home; and on the following week we set up a tent and sat in it while sharing our Bible story. Stories of the desert.

In the penultimate week of Lent, I sneaked into our classroom early and filled it up with stacking chairs. I posted a sign on the door that said: "*This room may not be used today. The church needs it for more important* COMMITTEE WORK." When the children arrived at the door of their desert home and found that it had been commandeered for "more important" purposes, they were angry and disappointed. What were those grown-ups thinking? This room was *our* desert! Committee things were not more important than our Jesus storytelling!

We walked into the room. We pushed back the chairs that were blocking the door. We surveyed our holy place. At last I said, "Maybe it was like this when Jesus walked into the temple and found that people had turned the church into a money-changing place. Remember how mad he was?" The children began to suspect I might be the perpetrator with my church school teacher motives. But the conversation that followed was very animated and insightful. We got to the story from the inside. With our imaginations.

Imagination is a key ingredient in a life of faith. Many of us would chafe to hear that said, lest we sound as if we are making up things that have no basis in experience, fact, or science. But what is imagination, anyway, but the ability to live an inside reality that is different from what our major senses are telling us in the moment? It is an expansion of boundaries. All of daily living involves our imagination – to foresee what comes next if I take a certain action, to imagine how my listener will interpret what I say, to see the possibilities that exist in situations, to love what can't be seen by the eyes alone. Children's ability to imagine possibilities is limited by their lack of life experience. But, adults' ability to imagine possibilities is limited by that very life experience – our expectation that what has happened before will simply happen again.

Mary Jo Leddy once said that the Word of God is found not in the Writings nor in the reading, but rather in the space between those sharing them. It is the interaction of the storyteller and the receiver that forms a bridge for Truth, a fluid space for the Spirit to hover. I love this description, especially because it seems to me that this was why Jesus chose to share spiritual truths in story, rather than in a systematic theology course.

If we are the raw materials that the Spirit turns into the Word of God, then both the song *and* the singing are a kind of sacrament. The actual meaning of the song will be very important – its words, its rhythm, melody and flow. Of equal importance will be the way we sing it – the context of our singing, the memories that are embedded for each of us within the song, the feeling we allow ourselves to express (or not), as well as the way in which we relate to each other in making the music. It is this meeting place of the song and the singing (or the story and the telling) that children inhabit so well. That I love best.

I became a song leader almost from the first moment I set foot in a church in my teens. In a gathering of people who claimed as part of their vocation the pouring out of their lives to God in song, I found a place and permission to do the same, along with a surprise – that the joy of helping ordinary seekers find their own voice surpassed even the profound satisfaction of singing and being heard on my own. Still today, I can think of little that rivals the exhilaration of leading of a group of women, men, teens, and little children in singing their own sound within a jumbled choir of jubilation.

I have found children to be very willing to dig into the words and meaning of a song or a story. Though their answers in the early years often mirror exactly what they have been taught by adults, it is their delight in the questions themselves and their willingness to probe for answers that is so inspiring to me. Robert Coles, who has worked with children around the world, said in *The Spiritual Life of Children* that he has found children to be "seekers… young pilgrims well aware that life is a finite journey and as anxious to make sense of it as those of us who are farther along in the time allotted us."

So, I have always made room for conversation to be a part of the process of song-creation. Most of the songs that I have written for children have emerged from an interchange I have had with a child, and some have even been written with children as co-composers.

Children are built – perhaps for survival purposes – with strong internal radar for the emotional content of adult words. This makes them particularly perceptive about the places where what is said does not line up with the way in which it is delivered. A slow song about the power of Pentecost is hard to believe, as is a choir deliberately and loudly proclaiming an otherwise gentle invitation to prayer. The emotional content of the song or story should be conveyed in the piece itself. Here's where the conversation about the song can be critical. When children understand what they are singing, they are amazing performers – in the truest sense. And the Word of God is spoken.

Asking children to chant the refrain, "O Dry Bones, hear the word of God!" as the bones noisily become living bodies, or singing "You can't come in, you can't come in; WE got here first!" as Jesus allows the paralytic man to be lowered through the ceiling, can catapult the whole group straight into the heart of the story. In my concerts, when children – and a couple of brave adults – do join me at the front of the church, God is bringing alive the very words that we sing: "I am amazing! I am filled with power! And God loves me like crazy!"

Singing and sharing in stories should be the easiest part of worshipping in a multi-age community. But it isn't. Choosing the particular stories and songs often creates a debate. Of course what we really yearn for, for ourselves and for our children, is a profound experience of ownership of the faith – of the stories, language, traditions, the lived experience of Christ's presence among us. But while we treasure the songs of our heritage and seek to pass them on to all who follow, we also need to look at the ways we are asking children to translate *themselves* in order to allow our language to make sense in their world.

Our response to this in the past has been to write music that was specifically designed for one age-group or another, and to live with the necessary separation. We created a "Time with the Children" with a children's hymn to end it, and returned to the order of service when they left. But, here's the funny part: the languages of children are not so different from the languages of adults. For example, a child's need for concreteness, rather than abstractness, is shared by many – or perhaps even most – adults.

As I compose, I try to create music of faith that speaks a variety of languages at the same time – line by line, phrase by phrase. One verse of *Singing Hallelujah* is this:

> Jesus had powers and they said he was a king *(a concrete image)*
> He turned all the tables on everything *(a concrete, real event – the temple table-turning scandal – and at the same time, the abstract image of Jesus changing our perceptions about everything that matters).*

I think we need to become more deliberate about creating, encouraging, and finding music that does this for the adult-to-young translation, as our times of worship with all ages increases.

I have also discovered a safety-catch for myself: In my own tendency to savour the art of beatific liturgical circumlocution, I can sometimes say things even *I* don't understand. The language covers for me! I have concluded that if I am not able to articulate a theological concept in the language of a five-year-old, I have not grasped the thing myself. (I suggest this breathalyzer for anyone seeking to share the faith!)

One of my all-time favourite discoveries in working with children and youth in the area of faith music, is that youth like the old words "thee" and "thou." In a youth consultation on hymns old and new, the gathering voted that they would prefer that old hymns keep the character of their old texts, without attempting to patch the old wineskins with new "you's."

I agree with them; the "updates" serve only to pretend the rest of the hymn actually speaks the language of this millennium. It doesn't – and this is okay. Yes, where hymns will continue to be sung by the community as a valid expression of Christian faith, their words will need to change to reflect an increasingly globally-sensitive understanding of the gospel. If that can be done while respecting the character and the poetry of their time, then I think we will be left with something that will last.

The thing is, the Tradition belongs to all of us – young and old. And while some things are predictable, such as youth's preference for high-intensity music, or the very small child's easy engagement with finger actions in a song, or the adult's need to see song lyrics written out, there are still surprises that continue to remind me of the fascinating and transformative voices through which God speaks.

By working with the song and the singing I get to see transformations take place at all levels. This morning, as I invited a group of 11-year-olds to play percussion together on a shared song, two boys whom I know to be from anxious homes told me they did not want to play. When I finally convinced them to take up a shaker part, the change was startling. One of them played with unaccustomed focus and energy; the other played with such intensity that he literally was with us no more, caught up in a kinesthetic expression of something he would normally resist, and yet to which – for one brief musical moment – he allowed himself to yield.

I feel my own participation in the tradition of the church enriched when I am able to share it with young people – and am surprised again and again with how they connect with it. After leading a group in a musical presentation this year, I had a young teen named Jack approach to me to say: "Who knew that Latin was so cool?"

Sometimes the song has allowed me to take part in healing quite beyond my own expectations or even intentions. A six-year-old refugee from the Middle East thanked me for writing "Like Iraq," when the song was actually "Like a Rock" (...God is under our feet"). Her so-called mis-hearing was a reminder to me that the Spirit often gives us just what we need, in the way we can best hear it.

I have also had the privilege of playing a part in the work of others for the healing of the world. Eight-year-old Alexandra wrote to me to ask if she might make use of my song, "O Great Earth" in the multi-media presentation she had been working on all year about Global Climate Change. She said, "I hope you say yes, because I love that song. I think it is perfect for my presentation and I hope my presentation makes people want to save this green and blue earth."

Recently, I was in the studio with a group of squiggly children, who had been invited to help me record a song on my new album. They stopped their jockeying just long enough for the tape to begin rolling. To our adult amazement, their wrestling gave way to melody as they sang with less-than-perfect tone yet perfect conviction: "Blest be this table for all... For all, for all... Blest be this table for all." There came a moment when the previously recorded adult voices re-joined, to a different line: "Blessed are those who are called to the table..." It brought tears to my eyes to hear the children hold their part, sailing above the voices that had gone before them, affirming in their own voices again and again: "Blest be this table for all."

Will anyone join me on this mountaintop?

Note: The songs referred to come from Linnea Good's albums: "Like a Rock" (co-written with Keri Wehlander), "I Am Amazing," and "O Great Earth" are from *Swimmin' Like a Bird* (for childlike spirits). "Blessed Are Those Who Are Called to the Table" is from *Momentary Saints* (for adult-like spirits). They, along with the unrecorded "Singing Hallelujah," are all available in *The Good Book*.

About the author

Linnea Good (www.LinneaGood.com) is a song & hymn-writer from Summerland, British Columbia. With a Master of Religious Education degree, she is a leader in the field of music and worship for all ages. She tours much of the year with her trio Good Company (including her drummer-husband and often their three young children), giving concerts, leading workshops and worshipping throughout North America. The latest of her numerous CDs, *Swimmin' Like a Bird*, was nominated for three major Canadian awards as Outstanding Children's Album of the Year. Linnea is co-author of *Adventures of the God Detectives*, published by Wood Lake Publishing Inc.

Art and Faith – Twinned in Spirit

Sally Armour Wotton

Once upon a time, long, long ago, there were costumed dancers, musicians and storytellers who carried our religious stories and celebrated creation quite naturally in worship. In the Western world, theatre was born in the church as a means of telling the gospel stories to a largely illiterate audience. This was the medieval period – a time of literal and unquestioning faith when one's belief in God and religious doctrines were intrinsic to daily life. The transition from this simple, assumed faith to the storm of religious argument in the 1600s drove the theatre out of the church and into the secular world where it could explore BIG issues and ideas freely. Only in the last century has theatre begun to make inroads back into the church, and it still meets with political difficulties when attempting to be at all radical (or Jesus-like).

My professional background was in New York theatre, and my ministry for the past thirty years has been as a performing arts event facilitator through my company, Sacred Acts. I have been the director of drama for a large Anglican church – St. John's York Mills – in Toronto for the past 24 years, preparing both youth and adults to present full-length productions and short dramas in worship. We have dramatized the scripture, done reflective dramas on the theme of the gospel, and offered drama as the sermon. We have even dramatized elements of liturgy, such as the sharing of the peace, to help make it better understood as a moment to come together in acceptance of our differences, rather than an opportunity to say, "Hi, how about a game of golf this weekend?"

Dramatizing scripture is the simplest way to include drama in worship; with most biblical stories, the script is already there. However, even when well read, the text creates a barrier between the reader and the "audience." Telling the story or using a small group of people to play the parts brings the characters and plot to life. I've received comments such as: "I've heard that story read hundreds of times in my life, but never really heard it until the group presented it this morning," and, "Telling the story instead of reading it made me feel I was there, that I was a part of the crowd – it was very moving," and, "I've always found the story of Abraham and Isaac so powerful, but seeing it enacted by a child and an older couple made me feel it in my gut."

The key to successful drama in worship is simplicity. Having a good narrator who can "save" the actors by saying the line they have forgotten or bringing them back to the text when they have jumped ahead is especially valuable with inexperienced actors. And in many cases, miming props is just as effective as using something tangible. Denoting characters by using a vivid coloured accessory rather than a full costume is also effective. Instead of interrupting the flow of worship by moving furniture, I have found long pieces of sari or lining fabric can literally flow into and out of a drama, representing both concrete and abstract concepts. Recently, in an enactment of St. John's Passion on Good Friday, a length of red fabric was used to illustrate a recurring theme. First, it was used as the cord that bound Jesus when he was sent off to Caiphas, then as Pilot's flowing mantle, and finally as the cross dragged down the centre aisle by Jesus.

There are many parallels between an actor's training and the skills needed for grace-filled living. Theatre/acting is always about taking risks. In fact, all artists must risk following where their intuitions and deepest thoughts lead them. Acting and faithful living are about trusting fellow players, because theatre, like life, is an art offered together with others. And acting is about discipline. Neither faith nor art is well served by dilettantes. Both require dedicated effort and daily exercise. But most importantly, acting is about relationships and self-discovery. Ralph Richardson said, at age 80, "I'm just beginning to get the hang of acting – discovering who I am."

Doing drama in church affords innumerable opportunities not only for discovering who we are but also for encountering our fellow worshippers in deeper, more meaningful ways. Working together to dramatize an important story is an intense experience. Recently, St. John's produced C.S. Lewis' *The Lion, The Witch and The Wardrobe* at a theatre near the church. We did it with live actors but created shadow puppets to enact the battle scenes. I had produced this play 18 years ago in the church itself. During that earlier production, two young adult players met, fell in love and married. At this most recent performance, one of the cast was the 16-year-old daughter of the "young" couple, and as she put it, "If it hadn't been for the earlier production of this show, I wouldn't have existed to play a role in this one." So theatre is about relationships both on and off stage!

The arts constitute a basic language in our lives, are essential to all lives and can be found in all lives. Art is the food for our creative imaginations – our spiritual sustenance. God is not creative: God is creativity itself. To play with earthy substance, movement, or words is to be in dialogue with God. Through art we ask our deepest questions, attempting to peel back the known to discover the unknown. When we have our small but vital "Ah Ha!" experiences we are, at those moments, engaged in active faith most fully.

For me, one such "Ah Ha!" experience was years ago during an Easter Passion performance. Mary was at the foot of the cross. Suddenly, the words from Luke recited at Christmas came flooding back to me, "And Mary treasured all these words and pondered them in her heart." And I felt, not merely heard, the mother's full realization of the meaning of those words she had held so long, and I wept. Perhaps it is at those moments of inspiration or revelation that we encounter the Holy Spirit.

The artist in me usually expresses herself through drama, writing or storytelling, but we are all storytellers when we share the events of our day with family or friends. I am not a photographer, and yet I occasionally take a very decent photo; I'm not a singer, but I love singing and burst out with my favourite songs from time to time. I'm certain that the same is true for us all: we are all capable of doing art. In the church, we need to recognize the artist in ourselves, hone our artistic leanings through some studying and rehearsing, and then share our efforts in order to spark a discussion or inspire a group of people to become a part of a gospel story and experience it afresh with us.

Art by definition has always been the process rather than the result. We can make it participatory so that it serves a need greater than the individual artist's/composer's/ playwright's vision. Increased participation has been the aim of the church's liturgy for the past 40 years. Artist and audience (congregation) can be partners; they can play together.

Imagination and play are essential elements for creating moments that invite participation. A number of years ago, when my husband and I were consumed with our fledgling careers and our son was young, we all felt the need for a holiday – a time to stop, relax, and enjoy one another's company. Ernest and I both worked from home, so we were always at work. We thought it would be good for Christopher to experience another country, but in addition to the fact that we couldn't afford to travel, it was February, the middle of the school year and, as always, the middle of work deadlines. It was a particularly rotten February, and we were feeling trapped in our apartment. One morning the radio was playing a catchy Jamaican number and when it ended, the host, who had visited Jamaica, began to laud it as a haven for the weary, and a playground for all. Christopher said, "Let's go!" First, we all laughed. Then we stopped, thought, and creative imagination kicked in. "Let's have a Jamaican weekend… in Toronto."

We made a trip to the library for illustrated books of Jamaica, and a visit to the travel agent for brochures. We borrowed some recipes and some reggae recordings from a Jamaican friend. Then we turned up the heat and unplugged the phone. Ernest rummaged around in the storage room and found a sun lamp saying, "If we've got to do this, we may as well come back with a tan."

Finally, and most importantly, we covered all our windows with orange, yellow and red tissue paper. We couldn't see the snow and ice outside, and the light came streaming through in brilliant colours. Then we relaxed, read, played, and wrote postcards made from travel brochure pictures. We forced ourselves to stop, for just a few days, to have childlike fun, and to be refreshingly unproductive. Drama at its most relaxing!

It would be interesting for a church group (or a whole church community) to try this for a day. You could choose a theme and transform a space in the church, providing "food" for all the senses, but no set program – just enter in and be. To do this would take courage and trust in creative imagination, but I think creative imagination is the Spirit acting through us. The group's reflection in the context of a simple service of prayer a week or two later could make the whole experience both worshipful and a work of art.

Art is the process of creating – of saying yes to life. When the artistic process becomes a completed painting, poem, composition, performance or event/experience, the art becomes a point of reflection for the artist and audience. Paul Klee, the German/Swiss abstract painter, would look at his canvasses after they were painted and give them a name. There is an element of Genesis in this process, reminding us of God inviting humanity to give names to the animals. This step of looking at one's own work and naming it is the last step of creation. It is also the first deed of response. The artist begins to react to his or her work in the process of reflecting and interpreting.

Faith is a similar quest for an experience and interpretation of God. When faith stops at creed or doctrine and is "carved in stone," it becomes static, non-living. Creeds or doctrines need to be used for reflection and interpretation so that the journey can continue. Out of this reflection will come new work – and, sometimes, renewed faith.

With our minds, bodies, and imaginations, we search for the source of creation. We are willing to risk much, if not all, to enter into this creative process, this chaos – when we let go of self for a time in order to be inspired through the possibility of glimpsing the sacred. This is the task of the artist in all of us, and this is the challenge of faith.

About the author

Sally Armour Wotton trained and worked in theatre in New York City throughout the 1960s. She is an adjunct professor in drama at Trinity College, University of Toronto, author of *Staging the Story* (a basic resource in liturgical drama) and founder of Sacred Acts – a consortium of artists who facilitate performing arts events for worship, education or the workplace across Canada.

The Singing Thing

John L. Bell

One week at Iona Abbey, there was a seminar based on the biblical
story of the call of Samuel (1 Samuel: 1). The leader made the point...
that the voices we hear when we are young reverberate in us throughout
our lives, sometimes enabling or disabling us in particular activities.

The group – a very diverse mixture of academics, consultants, house-
wives and artisans – were asked to describe the voices which they personally heard echoing through the corridors of time into their present existence. It was a very revelatory moment, as one by one people recounted
the voices and phrases that still belittled them.

One man said he kept hearing a particular person calling him a 'Jessie'
because as a youth he had been slightly effeminate. An author said she still
heard a teacher's voice calling her 'a proper little madam.' A doctor said that
he was haunted by his grandmother's voice saying, 'You'll never be as good
as your father.' And others recounted how they would be about to sketch a
map to show a friend how to get from A to B when they would hear an art-
master's voice proclaiming, 'You can't draw!' It became transparent that no
matter how sophisticated, cultured, articulate or capable people are in their
adult lives, the voices they heard in their childhood can still disable them.

It is exactly the same for those who believe they cannot sing because
someone once told them so. Across the years the pronouncement of doom
reverberates...It is as if the memory takes an audio-visual recording of the
incident which can be action-replayed at the drop of a hat. Something inside instinctively informs us that from this moment on our life will be different. The person who has been so much a part of us is no longer. We are
bereft of someone who was vital to us and we are helplessly diminished...

I remember standing next to a Roman Catholic priest during a liturgy
in Northern Ireland. After the service, I said to the priest, 'It's good to
stand beside a man who actually sings at mass.'

'Oh, I don't sing,' replied the priest, 'I can't. I'm tone deaf.'

'Not at all!' I protested. 'There were three hymns plus a psalm and the
Sanctus and you sang every one of them.'

'You're just saying that to make me feel good,' he said.

'Listen, I'm not making out that you're Pavarotti. But I want you to know that you sang all through mass and that you sang in tune.'

But still he would not believe it.

There is a remedy for such people, for the vast majority of those who believe they can't sing, and it does not involve a long course of psycho-analysis or training in vocal technique. It has to do with renaming and decision-making. But before elaborating on these, here [is a testimony] from the self-confessed tone deaf.

Andrew's story

Andrew was in his sixties. He had worked in religious broadcasting most of his life.

At an Advent carol service one year he was asked if he had enjoyed the service.

'All except the singing,' he replied.

'What was wrong with the singing?' asked his friend.

'I can't sing,' he responded.

'Who told you?' his friend enquired.

'Miss Brown.'

'When was this?'

'Oh it was a while ago.' And then he recounted with great accuracy the precise moment:

'We were in music class. It was a Friday afternoon. I was sitting at the back beside Alex MacAskill. We were singing a folk song, a border bal-lad. I think it was *March, March, Ettrick and Teviotdale*. Suddenly Miss Brown stopped playing the piano and began to speak directly to me.

'She said, "Andrew Sloan, would you just mime please. You're putting the other boys off." So I've never sung from that day to this.'

Asked when exactly that had happened, Andrew replied, 'I remember that the windows in the music room were painted round the edges of the glass. And I remember it had big dark curtains. So it must have been dur-ing the blackout in the war. Maybe about 1940–41.'

'And what age was Miss Brown?'

'She'd probably have been about 26. All the older male teachers had got called up to the army.'

His friend then pointed out to Andrew, that he, a man approaching seventy, was allowing his singing voice to be held ransom by a woman who was less than half his age.

He had never looked at it that way...

Dozens of similar stories could be told, all of which have the common denominator of a person in authority or a loved friend or relative telling the individual at a young or transitional stage in their life that they couldn't sing.

Because the accused could not argue against the criticism, they believed it. Because no one has persuasively contradicted the opinion, they believe it twenty or thirty or fifty years later.

What is the remedy?

Renaming and decision-making are the essential means to recovery.

Renaming

When people are told they can't sing, they feel that there is a label round their neck or a mark on their file indicating a permanent disability.

What they need to do is move from that negative assumption or label to a positive one. And this transition is a very biblical thing, because God is in the renaming business. Abram becomes Abraham, Sarai becomes Sarah – and this because the new name indicates a more positive state of being. It comes when they agree to be liberated by God from the sterility which surrounds them.

In the Gospels, Jesus does the same thing. He takes Simon who is fully aware of his unreliability and, flying in the face of common sense, decides to call him Peter – the Rock, on which the Church is to be built. When confronted with a disfigured woman who would be called mad or diseased or something more impolite by her fellow citizens and their children, Jesus brings her into the middle of the synagogue and calls her 'a daughter of Abraham.'

Renaming is part of God's business. God delights to get rid of the rumours, nicknames and debilitating labels of the past. God identifies the potential rather than bemoaning the problematic.

So, whenever people refer to themselves as being tone deaf or tuneless, somehow they have to discover that theirs is a voice in the making, or a voice in the waiting. They have to realize that they are expected by God and the people of God to sing, irrespective of what they have heard or believed about themselves in the past.

And the people responsible for changing the name and the expectation are those who in the leadership of music and worship decide either to encourage all of God's people to praise their Maker with their voices, or who make it clear from their demeanour and conversation that they anticipate and desire only those who are musically 'gifted' to engage in song.

Church musicians, in God's name, have to rename all the self-confessed groaners as apprentice angels, and to believe that they will begin to sing.

Annette's story

The proof of the pudding can be found in the story of Annette, arguably one of the most vocally disadvantaged of women. Her voice wandered off and on pitch, and made a terrible rasping sound, no doubt aided and abetted by copious supplies of nicotine and a past history of alcoholism.

She attended a weekend conference for church musicians where it was put to her that she had the voice of an apprentice angel – something which she clearly doubted. But over the weekend she engaged in every seminar, tried songs she had never sung before, and began to exhibit a quiet self-confidence.

Three weeks later, Annette phoned the conference leader to ask if he would come to her church one Friday to help a group of people to pray. She explained that many were struggling with poverty or addiction or emotional traumas and that Friday night was a safe evening for these folk in a safe place.

When the leader arrived, quite at sea as to what to do in a situation which was alien to him, he was met by Annette who informed him: 'You don't have to worry about the singing thing. They can all do it. I taught them the Russian *Kyrie* in three parts the way you taught me. I just said to them, "Listen, I have been told that I have the voice of an apprentice angel. And if I can make music, all of you can."'

She then took her friend into a room where everybody's face told of a history of sadness, marginalization or abuse. And to his astonishment she began to get them to sing in three parts the Orthodox *Kyrie*…He did not have to do much to enable them to pray. They were halfway there, thanks to the efforts of a husky-throated woman who took on a new name for herself.

We develop by growing into the fullness of life God intends for us, not by repeating the limiting labels of the past which diminish us.

Decision-making

The other part of the remedy has to do with decision-making.

The conversation in which Andrew Sloan told his friend how Miss Brown had pronounced the death sentence on his voice during a wartime music class led the friend to say to Andrew, 'For you to sing you have to make a choice, a theological choice. Who is bigger? Miss Brown, who was less than half your age when she told you that you couldn't sing, or God, who says to you, "Sing me a new song"?'

For it is perfectly possible that the Miss Browns of the world were ignorant as regards male teenage voice development. It is possible that the Miss Browns were motivated in their comments more by a dislike of teenage boys than by discerning judgment about adolescent voices. It is also possible that the Miss Browns just got it wrong...

[For] when God asks us to sing a new song, it is because God believes that we can...

(A congregation's story)

What is true for individuals in this respect is true also for congregations. We discovered this when two of us spent some time attached to a church in an Urban Priority Area in Glasgow.

The congregational singing was dire. Worse still, several people in the congregation were keen to tell us that 'this is the church that can't sing'. Every Sunday they evidently stood up to prove it.

What had happened was that somewhere in the distant past, which no one could specifically identify, either a musician or a minister had let the congregation know that it did not sing well. The whole community, hearing this word from an 'authority,' took it seriously as a pronouncement on its abilities, and from that time onwards became reticent to sing.

When we began to work in the church, we met a group of twelve people every Thursday evening, to look at the worship life of the congregation and to discern ways in which it could be enlivened.

Only one of these twelve people could read music; the rest all presumed that they couldn't sing. So we began each Thursday evening meeting with twenty minutes in which we simply sat and sang. We sang favourite hymns, children's hymns, and gradually introduced new songs which were going to be included in church services.

After four months, not only did this small group of twelve people sing confidently, but the whole congregation were singing better, because of the presence in it of twelve people who had begun to believe in their own voices.

The objective proof of improvement came when a woman who had left the church two years previously to live in the Scottish Highlands came back to visit her daughter and to attend morning worship. 'I couldn't believe my ears,' she said. 'The last time I went to that church, it was like a congregation of tailor's dummies. But last Sunday they sang like linties (thrushes).'

Here, again, it was not a matter of lecturing the people or employing any slick recuperative technique. It was simply changing their self-perception from the church that couldn't sing to the church that could, and allowing people to believe in their own voices...

In the West we are going into uncharted territory where music is increasingly seen as something which is the preserve of gifted individuals whom others are expected to listen to and admire. The more this aspect of musical culture prevails, the less will ordinary people perceive that it is their prerogative to sing and participate in communal music-making. Therefore when the Church invites people to sing hymns, it is doing something profoundly counter-cultural. It is both presuming that all can sing, and providing material specifically written so that the whole community can participate.

About the author

The Rev. John L. Bell is an ordained minister of the Church of Scotland and a member of the Iona Community, where he develops resources in the areas of music and worship with the Wild Goose Resource Group. He has produced many collections of original hymns and songs (some in collaboration with Graham Maule) and two collections of songs of the world church. As an expression of the Iona Community's commitment to the renewal of public worship in the Christian church, the Wild Goose Resource Group exists to renew traditions of song and worship, Christian education, and faith commitment in a modern context.

PART 5

Transforming
How We Learn

The imagination is the creative force in the individual. It always negotiates different thresholds and releases possibilities of recognition and creativity that the linear, controlling, external mind will never even glimpse. The imagination works on the threshold that runs between light and dark, visible and invisible, quest and question, possibility and fact. The imagination is a great friend of possibility. Where the imagination is awake and alive, fact never hardens or closes but remains open, inviting you to new thresholds of possibility and creativity.

— JOHN O'DONOHUE, ANAM CARA: A BOOK OF CELTIC WISDOM

Dancing with Words

Ray Buckley

It was her shoes that I always noticed first. They seemed much too large and heavy for such a small person. Still, they had carried her feet for many miles and must have seemed like old, trusted friends. They bore the scars of rocks and brush and the occasional pavement that had attempted to thwart their determined destiny.

From where I sat on the ground, I could see that her brown stockings fell into friendly wrinkles that seemed to match those on her hands and arms and cheeks. It was as if everything about her was in agreement and assumed a comfortable position. Far below her knees, the hem of a cotton dress met the stockings. Careful washing had dulled its color, and it gracefully carried the even lighter shade of where her hands had rested on her knees over many years. Around and above her waist was a collection of rounded, gentle shapes that included several cotton bags filled with extraordinary surprises and a light shawl that served as cover and portable throne.

She was always slightly bent, but when she leaned over a child, one could see all of her journeys traced on her face. They ran softly around the chin and enveloped the ears. They meandered around her cheeks, leaving two smooth places. They found a home around her eyes and played there awhile before moving gently into the wisps of white hair that became a stream of braid down her back.

There was an enormous comfort to her. I loved the "coming-toward-me" side of her because it filled me with joy. There was a welcoming to her that seemed like a perpetual invitation. I do not choose to remember the "going-away" side as well because there was an empty spot in any place when she was no longer there.

She was named well. She was named after the black-tailed deer that lived in the grasslands. When she was young, her light form and large eyes must have brought to mind those small, delicate deer that hid in cottonwood tree groves. We called her "Grandma," not only because we called most elderly women

"Grandma" but also because she knew us all by name and could tell us the names of our ancestors and the adventures they had known. She knew the sacred stories and the comic ones. She knew stories of brave men and even braver women. She knew stories of the animals and Those That Crawled. She knew the stories of the First Beginnings. She kept stories like she kept the treasures in her bags. She wore them as comfortably as the shawl and stockings. Some seemed enormous and weighty, like her shoes.

There was a protocol to our listening. If we began talking, she would simply stop and walk away. The story may not have continued until days later. Some stories were selectively shared, waiting for the right moment or audience. They were, after all, a gift to be opened and delighted in, and gifts were chosen carefully. She watched our faces as the story-gifts were revealed, taking delight in our delight. We listened with ears and eyes, merging sight and sound into an almost tangible form. We listened for key words, which were emphasized by slowing the language, leaning forward, and asking with the eyes, "Did you hear it? Did you catch the importance?"

Her voice was soft. One had to listen intently. Seldom was it raised. Sometimes the words came quickly, sometimes slowly. There were moments when the story was moving at you. Sometimes she would pause and breathe in deeply, as if she were pulling you into the place where the story began. The sharing of the story was not without the sharing of self. The story had become part of the shoes and the brown stockings. It had become part of the soft wrinkles and the white braid.

From the first words, "This is my story...," we were drawn into the tale, as if those words were a cue for our brains to shift from the present reality into a place where we were feeling, smelling, and tasting the world of the story. Her eyes, voice, smile, hands, and posture conveyed countless pieces of nonverbal information. She chose her words carefully, like one would choose marbles from a glass jar. Silence itself was a chosen word-turned-paragraph. A gesture, frozen in midair, became an exclamation point. She was a dancer whose legs no longer moved well. She painted with colors we saw in our minds. She was a weaver of *words, handing one a basket woven of thought. But when it was complete the basket became ours.*

I have a collection of these baskets in my memory. They are part of my mind and spirit. They have become woven into my psyche. They were the gift of the storyteller as we wove them together – her stories and our imaginations. The concepts have broadened as I have become older. Many of the characters have become metaphors. Many of the words have developed into ideas. The morals have influenced my behavior. The values have become part of who I am.

We became a community, those of us who listened. We were united by story. We were united by imagery. We had a moment of combined history and imagination. The words bound us to our cultures. The experiences of the characters became our experiences brought to life by the storyteller. She "breathed to life" the story and in doing so breathed the same life into a part of us.

Growing up, I would listen to our Lakota elders speaking of their life experiences. In the stories they told and in the way they greeted each other were three beautiful words heard over and over. In her beautiful book *Bead on an Anthill: A Lakota Childhood* (University of Nebraska Press, 1998), Delphine Red Shirt placed them together. Seeing those words together, almost like a poem, has placed them indelibly in my memory. I never think of them apart from one another.

Weksuye (Wek [*e* as in they]-soo-yeh) – I remember
Ciksuye (Cik [*c* as in chair, *i* as in mill]-soo-yeh) – I remember you
Miksuye (Mik [*i* as in mill]-soo-yeh) – Remember me

Somewhere in the process of storytelling, the story becomes memory. If the story has connected with our spirits, then that memory is the gift of the storyteller. We are able to say: I remember. This is a part of me. These are things of importance to me. This collective experience of storytelling has been internalized into collective memory. The visual images are the ones we share. *Weksuye. I remember.*

I remember you. I remember how you moved and spoke. I remember the things you did, the words you chose, and how you believed. I remember the essence of who you were. I remember you, though we were generations apart. You have become part of my active memory and have impacted the things that I celebrate, enjoy, and believe. I remember you, because others remembered you and kept you alive. *Ciksuye. I remember you.*

Remember me. I tell you of the things I feel and have experienced. They are part of who I am. When the living reminders of my life have passed on, these are the songs, words, events, prayers, actions, joys, sorrows, triumphs, defeats, dances, and solitary moments that have been a part of me. These things have become part of the story. If they have value for you, in whatever time and place you find yourself – remember me. *Miksuye. Remember me!*

We choose to remember for the purpose of sharing stories. Storytelling affirms for us the memory of our people, whoever they may be. Long before the written word or the printing press, those who first told and remembered the stories passed on a legacy as human beings. We are people of the story, and we seek to identify and tell our stories in nearly everything we do...

Storytellers in any traditional community serve as culture bearers. Within our stories are contained elements of our cultures that we wish to transmit to other generations. Our primary purpose is not to entertain but to continue culture. Storytellers in faith-based communities share that same purpose. We are sharing the stories, and creating stories, that contain the essence of what we believe. Our primary purpose is to share and continue our faith. There is a reason why we tell stories, and a reason why we tell the stories we do.

There is also a reason why we choose storytelling as a vehicle of culture. Storytelling is personal contact. The sharing of faith at its best is personal. Storytelling is an effective means of communication for both large and small groups, as well as for multi- or single-generational audiences. Though we have moved away from it to a degree, sharing our faith through the use of story is one of our earliest traditions.

Storytelling in communities of faith serves a teaching function. The storyteller must be accurate to the source and, in many cases, to the tradition. The storyteller then becomes a scholar (at the very least, a dedicated student) of her or his faith and its tradition. To a larger degree, the storyteller becomes an interpreter of that faith.

As storytellers in faith communities we must know our cultures, be careful in how we interpret those beliefs through story, be accurate to our sources, and inspire faith.

There is also another important ingredient. We must believe. We must be credible in our personal faith.

Would you allow me to be personal for a moment? When I was younger I did not feel comfortable with the designation "storyteller." A good portion of those feelings came from the extraordinary storytellers I knew. To me, stories had a sacred function, and people who shared them were larger than life. Storytellers were heroic. I am not exactly certain that they would have called themselves storytellers. They would have been comfortable with "culture bearers" or "keepers of tradition." Modesty would have prevented them from assuming a claim to any skills or accomplishment. They were story-keepers.

In Lakota tradition, individuals were granted the right to tell stories because they embodied the values of that particular story in their own lives. They were, and are, living stories.

Most of the stories I tell are true. That is a prejudice on my part, because the people I have known have been remarkable people. When I tried to talk with others about the people who have impacted my life, I was telling their stories. As I have spoken about them, certain aspects of their lives and characters have become solidified in my thinking. Hindsight also gave me the ability to see the movement of God in my life through other people. As I spoke the words about their lives, the values they had taught me became clearer. Each time that I "spoke those beliefs into being" my life changed as I shared the stories of others.

There was also another unsuspected thing that took place. As I shared the words and the experiences, they impacted my life to such a degree that I made conscious decisions to commit to many of those same beliefs. Stories had become an opportunity for spiritual growth. I not only believed but also was practicing those beliefs. I was affirming the legacy of faith. The discipline of sharing stories enabled me to look at my own life experiences as a story. I was startled by the many answered prayers, the orchestration of events, and the unmistakable reality of God in my life. I prayed more. I celebrated the lives of others more. And I looked for God in unexpected places.

I had become part of The Story.

When we engage the stories that are part of our traditions, like all others before us, they have the power to impact our lives. The difference is, we live in them. We wrap them around ourselves and become warm. We share that warmth. There is not a way to step into the water of faith stories without becoming wet. When we do step in, it challenges our faith, our commitment, and the way we choose to live. It is supposed to.

Here, I believe, is why...The story [is] a living being and...when it touches the spirit of another, [it] lives...It [has] potential for uplifting someone, for offering hope or empowerment. Here is an essential element of my faith. When we encounter spiritual truth, whether in a story or casual conversation, we encounter the Living God, ready for relationship. At every turn, we discover God. We do not cause it. It happens because we are willing to tell the story. Someone meets God.

Is the Spirit of God present with us when we tell stories of faith? I believe so. With all my heart, I believe so. Is the Spirit of God with us only as we share stories of faith? No, with all my heart I believe that the Spirit of God delights in revealing God in surprising places and blessing our lives in all that we do. Still, for clergy and laity, young and old, formally educated and life-student, there is a desire to tell *The Story*. At times, the testimonies of those who have gone before us and the presence of God seem tangible, and the words flow beyond our capabilities. Someone listens and hears with new ears. There is an anointing of those who tell stories and those who sing and those who bake bread and give it away. We are rediscovering those things.

When I was younger, I was not comfortable with being called a storyteller. Now I am older, and even more so than when I was young, I stand in awe at the power of stories. I am not willing to be called a storyteller, for I am still a student. But I cannot stop, for there is much to tell and so many reasons to do so. I am one who heard *The Story*, and it changed my life. I cannot stop telling others about it.

About the author

Ray Buckley is the former director of the Native People's Communications Office for United Methodist Communications. He is the author of *Dancing with Words: Storytelling as Legacy, Culture, and Faith*, and the author/illustrator of four other books: *God's Love Is Like..., The Give-Away: A Christmas Story in the Native American Tradition, The Wing*, and *Christmas Moccasins*.

Cosmic Zoom and Galactic Weeds

Tim Scorer

Imagine your body, free of rockets and spaceship, lifting off from earth and heading out into space. As you watch earth grow smaller behind you, the moon, the sun, and the planets of our solar system slide past. You're moving so fast that millions of other suns of the Milky Way, our galactic home, go by and become a vast cosmic field of light spots – and you see the entirety of our galaxy glowing solitary and whole in space. Then, you're zooming past millions of other galaxies on a journey that takes you to the very edge of the universe, where you slow down, stop, and begin the return journey all the way back to the spot on planet earth where you began – standing next to a boy on whose arm the proboscis of a mosquito is extracting blood. Now you begin the other journey. You've had the macro, now you're off into the micro, taking the cosmic journey into one of those drops of blood and zooming through a universe of molecules and atoms until you reach the edge of that universe, slow down and come back to where you began – next to a boy, on his floating home in space, being stung by a mosquito.

That's the scenario of an artistic and scientific treasure from The National Film Board of Canada – a short animated film called *Cosmic Zoom* that was made in 1968. It was light years ahead of its time in the way that it wordlessly presented the two realities between which we live our day-to-day sensate existence: the infinite magnitude of space, and the ultimate minuteness of matter. I think that those eight minutes of animated wonder had a huge impact on the shaping of my cosmic and spiritual consciousness. I've noticed a number of times over the years how that little animated act of human creativity provided me with a frame of reference for the sacred mystery of cosmic creativity, both vast and intimate.

One of those times happened quite recently when I was planning a small group study session based on Bruce Sanguin's book *Darwin, Divinity, and the Dance of the Cosmos*. We were looking at the chapter that had us examining our evolutionary journey that began in a great creative flaring forth 13.7 billion years ago, and continues in the startling reality of an ever-expanding universe. As I thought of ways to bring the participants in the group to a place of cosmic wonder, I recalled my own sense of awe at the images of deep space that had been made accessible to us through the Hubble Telescope. I began to imagine creating a gallery of deep space images of galaxies and stars – a gallery into which I could invite the participants as part of the evening session. Where would I find my gallery?

Rather than cutting up a coffee-table book, I opted to find two calendars of Hubble images – 24 spectacular pieces of cosmic art. When I arrived at Oscar's, the bookstore with the best selection of calendars in Vancouver, I had no thought that anything would be required for the gallery other than the 24 Hubble images. However, Oscar's is one of those spirit-filled bookstores where serendipity rules. On this occasion my wife came across a book which was a visual spectacle to match the Hubble images, but at an entirely different level of cosmological existence: weeds! Howard Bjornson, a naturalist and photographer, had taken crystal clear photos of solitary weeds set against a plain backdrop, often black. There were amazingly sculpted pods, prickly seed heads, simply elegant flowers, slim grasses – all wonderful constellations of procreativity. In one bookstore moment the word "weed" was redefined! *Cosmic Zoom*, the animated film from the NFB, had prepared me for just such a moment: I instantly realized that the gallery I was planning had to be both the macro of space and the micro of weeds.

What I created for the group was a stunning visual adventure where galactic weeds took their place amongst the seedpods and spirals of deep space. I wondered at first if it was to be a silent gallery experience, but discovered that a CD of improvised cello music by David Darling was just the right kind of sound accompaniment for this meeting of seeds and galaxies.

It seems that sometimes we use the word "breathtaking" too casually. To have one's breath taken away by something so awesome that there can be no other response is actually remarkable. The response of the group members was of that kind. One member of the group commented, "What I loved about the gallery was seeing how, when juxtaposed, the shape of the galaxies and weeds mirrored one another. It filled me with a sense of awe. Seeing patterns reflected at the micro and macro level reminded me of the order that is inherent in chaos – a Divine order." Wordlessly and collectively, we lived the experience of recognizing that our existence is framed by infinite and untouchable magnitude as well as minute and infinitely touchable intimacy. It was quite simply another cosmic zoom!

As I drove home that evening, feeling overwhelmed by the sense of awe that had been opened through the images of galaxies and weeds, I found myself reflecting on the place of art experience in adult education. In such times of reflection, I find that I arrive at a reaffirmation of a truth that I first learned thoroughly in the context of drama in education, namely, that the creative arts have a power to "take us off guard" and to bypass our overdependence on language and thought. We could have spent the evening exercising our heads and voices by showing off our scientific knowledge of deep space; instead we took the risk of allowing image and music to open our hearts and minds to the wonder of our extraordinary galactic paradise. It is in such moments that we can truly feel the transformative power of our evolutionary universe moving through us.

About the author

Tim Scorer is an educator, writer, facilitator and spiritual director who lives on Bowen Island near Vancouver, British Columbia. With Wood Lake Publishing he creates small-group study curricula based on the books of scholars like Marcus Borg, John Dominic Crossan, and Bruce Sanguin. He also accompanies congregations and people in ministry in achieving their desire for effective, spirit-centered leadership.

The World's Most Dangerous Bible Study

Eric Elnes

During my first year at [Scottsdale Congregational United Church] we started a Wednesday Logos program for children and youth. Logos is an ecumenical, nationwide program that goes by different names in churches (ours is called B.E.A.C.H.). The basic program contains four elements: Bible study, worship skills, recreation, and dinner. The program is run primarily by laity.

Just before our program started, there was one gaping hole: no one had come forward to lead Bible study for our middle and high school youth. Since I had just arrived from Princeton Theological Seminary fresh from my Ph.D. studies in the Hebrew Bible, all heads turned to me. "Eric, how would you like to lead Bible study for the middle and high school groups?" someone asked. I was just naive enough at the time to answer, "Sure, I'd love to! I've never taught youth before. It sounds like fun."

I was pretty excited about the whole thing until I met the youth themselves and assessed their interest in, and commitment to, studying the Bible at somewhere less than zero! Panic set in.

I don't particularly like using prepackaged curricula to teach any form of class, but in this case I was so desperate I sorted through piles of published youth-oriented Bible studies. Much to my dismay, I found them to be utterly boring or overly conservative, or both. So I cleared them off my desk, got down on my knees, and prayed. Hard!

I asked God, "What is at the center of our youth's world?" I figured that if I could discern what was at the center, I could step into it, on their own turf, bringing scriptures along with me, letting them speak naturally within the world of our youth.

It didn't take me long to figure out that if anything is at the center, music is part of it – rock, pop, alternative, rap, even country music for some. Happily, at the time I was listening to much of the same music, which emboldened me to step into the center of their world using music as our common meeting place.

I started something that has become known as *The World's Most Dangerous Bible Study* (WMDBS). Each week we would focus on a particular song and one or two Scripture passages. My criteria for selecting a song were simple: (1) are the youth currently listening to it, and (2) does it express anything meaningful about life? Theologically, I assumed that if a song expresses anything meaningful about life, there must be a way of engaging with it fruitfully in Scripture.

Having selected a song, we would play it on a boom box (usually at high decibel levels!), following along with lyrics I had printed for the group in advance. When the song was over, I would ask, "What are the major thoughts, emotions, and messages you find in the song?" Responses would be written on a white board behind me.

Then we would turn to one or two Scripture passages I had chosen in advance. We would read each passage, then ask the same questions we had of the song, noting responses on the white board.

Finally, after discussing both the song and the scriptures in isolation, we would set them in conversation, asking, "What similarities and differences do we find between the song and the scriptures?"

The purpose of the WMDBS was not to say, "Look at your evil, devil music compared to the great and awesome scriptures." Nor was it to say, "You see, it all just says the same thing anyway (so why read the Bible?)." Rather, its purpose was to engage faith and everyday life using the Bible and popular music as conversation partners.

Can you imagine what happened? It worked! By "worked" I primarily mean three things:

1. The youth actually showed up each week, rather than every once in a while – when they had nothing "better" to do.
2. The youth often brought friends – sometimes even their "significant others."
3. Most important, the youth got it.

By "got it" I do not mean to imply that when they hear, say, Alanis Morissette's "You Learn" on the radio, they think of Romans 8:28–39, which I had paired with this particular song. Rather, I mean that when the youth hear a song we covered in the WMDBS, they remember. They remember that faith engaged the heart of their everyday lives in a fruitful way – in a way that mattered very personally to them.

About the author

Dr. Eric Elnes, is a biblical scholar with a Ph.D. from Princeton Theological Seminary. He is also Senior Pastor of Countryside Community Church (UCC) in Omaha, NE (www.countrysideucc.org). He is the author of *The Phoenix Affirmations: A New Vision for the Future of Christianity* (Jossey-Bass, 2006), *Asphalt Jesus: Discovering a New Christian Faith along the Highways of America* (Jossey-Bass, 2007) and *Igniting Worship: The Seven Deadly Sins*, which gives an in-depth look at his internationally recognized work in developing Incarnational Worship.

Shaping Shalom

Catherine Kapikian

In the early 1980s, Catherine Kapikian was invited to be artist-in-residence at Wesley Theological Seminary in Washington, DC. She never left.

In the ensuing years, with three major grants from the Henry Luce Foundation, and with the ongoing cooperation of more and more colleagues, she enabled a comprehensive integration and transformation of theological education through the arts. All students who come to Wesley Theological Seminary are not only required to take a course in the arts, but are also beneficiaries of an environment wherein the arts thrive. These include a working studio with resident artists; the opportunity for artistic expressions in response to academic requirements; challenging exhibits in a museum-quality gallery; forums integrating arts and theology, creative process and spiritual formation; chancel dramas; dance practicums; etc.

At our seminary, we have a tunnel that is 100' long and turns a corner. Everyone walks through this space, often to and from chapel services. The temperature drops upon entering the tunnel, and in the summer, mold creeps up its walls. Occasionally, the tunnel floods.

In the 1970s, an innovative student arrived one day with several gallon cans of paint purchased in a nearby hardware store. Thinking that her plan to paint Noah's ark in the tunnel was the perfect solution, she handed the $50 receipt for the paint to the academic dean. He balked, and she returned the paint.

In the 1980s, I petitioned the administration with a proposal to restore the walls and install lights to set off masterful ceramic relief sculptures of contemporary Stations of the Cross. They had been created and given to us by one of our artists-in-residence. This proposal would have enabled cast shadows resulting from directed lighting on the relief figures, progression of subject matter logically fitting the elongated space, the transformation of a dull space into a devotional space, and subtle physical discomfort induced by temperature change to be an asset in experiencing the thematic content of the stations. The solution was rejected due to lack of funds for lighting and minimal wall restoration.

In the 1990s Union Theological Seminary in Richmond, (Virginia), sent one of its students for a two-semester sojourn at our seminary. He was an accomplished studio artist and college professor of studio art seeking practical experience integrating art with theology. Woong-Sik Timothy Chon and I peered down the tunnel and schemed. By now, the community was ripe for a transformative change. The failed attempts of the past had left their imprints.

Knowing from past experience how critical having an informed community is, I appointed a small, select committee from the faculty, staff, and student body. I solicited a polished, in-scale, full-color design concept from Chon, fashioned after the two of us had experimented with and decided upon a buon fresco technique as the medium of expression. The committee accepted our concept. Chon began his arduous task surrounded by an inquisitive, caring community and lovingly supported by his wife and three small children.

As fall progressed, Chon created cartoons (preparatory drawings) that combined Eastern and Western influences and tackled the inherent problems in this exacting technique of applying paint to a perfectly prepared wall of wet lime and plaster. At the moment of control with this process, Chon was catapulted into the abyss. His daughter Soh-Leen Sarah Chon, following 100 days of life just celebrated at her baptism, died suddenly in her sleep. Wracked by pain, grief, and anguish Chon returned week after week to the tunnel. Sometimes he labored productively, other times in vain, and mostly in solitary sadness.

In these initial weeks, buckets of seemingly black paint bonded to the wall. Colleagues passed through the tunnel in silence. I teetered between trust in Chon's process, my responsibility as kind friend and mentor (Chon needed the therapeutic benefits of painting), and the committee's threshold for a work radically different from the one proposed. No one said a word as they passaged through the tunnel, and some averted their stares at the wall being painted. The kind of preparation discussed above stood all of us in good stead.

In the ensuing months, Chon transformed our tunnel into the visual epic journey of a person moving through grief to hope. He put before us a monumental work of abstracted imagery being testimony to God's healing presence. Traversing one side of the 100' tunnel from floor to ceiling and a portion of the opposing wall seen upon entering at its turned end, Chon moved the imagery through the following eight themes: creation, mother and child, marriage of heaven and earth, lament, transformation, resurrection, reunion, and text (a handsome calligraphic rendering of Matthew 11:5).[1] Near the solitary panel of text, mounted on the wall, is a shelf lacquered in the oriental red that repeats the color of the molding outlining the top and bottom edge of the whole fresco. On this shelf sits a large book of empty pages in which a steady stream of anonymous prayers and reflections appear. Now, the tunnel is a place of healing. This venture necessitated a creative response from the artist and community alike. Says Chon, "God used the creative process of the fresco painting to shape Shalom."

To this day, people passing through the tunnel leave a prayer, a petition filling the empty pages of the open book, a living testimony of the enduring power of this place. It has become a place of healing.

Note: the italicized paragraphs at the beginning and end of this piece were written by Catherine Kapikian specifically for this reprint. ·

About the author

Catherine Kapikian is founder and director of the pioneering Henry Luce III Center for the Arts and Religion at Wesley Theological Seminary in Washington, DC. She is a member of the faculty in the interdisciplinary field of art and theology. An acclaimed artist, her work, inclusive of paraments, vestments, banners, tapestries, and fiber with wood installations, can be seen in a variety of worship spaces in every major Christian denomination, as well as interfaith military chapels, and synagogues. Many of her large format works, like needlepoint tapestries behind altars, are designed by her and fabricated by members of the community in what she calls "participatory aesthetics." In this manner, the installation becomes the work of the people. In addition to teaching, giving workshops, and supervising resident artists at the Center, she writes and publishes articles in the field of art and theology.

---

[1] KARIN TUNNELL TRANSCRIBED THE SCRIPTURAL TEXT INTO A FULL-SCALE, CALLIGRAPHIC CARTOON FOR THE WALL AND ASSISTED CHON IN CARVING THE TEXT INTO THE WALL.

PART 6

Transforming Churches

Practice resurrection.
~ WENDELL BERRY, MANIFESTO: THE MAD FARMER LIBERATION FRONT

House of Mercy
A Ministry of Renewal through Worship, Theology, and the Arts

Bob Brusic

The sign on the stately Gothic church at the end of Ninth and Wacouta Streets said "The First Baptist Church of St. Paul." Built in 1875, the building is well kept, though standing in solitary splendor, alone on an island in the midst of the urban landscape. The church, with ten vintage stained-glass windows and an organ said to be the finest between Chicago and the west coast, has no visible residential neighborhood, just some empty lots and a highway off in the distance.

Approaching the church by automobile along Wacouta Street, it is easy to overlook the modest sign to the side that announces "House of Mercy." It was only after making a cell phone call that I realized that, despite the elusive signage, House of Mercy, known as an "alternative congregation," was housed in this building. When I eventually met Russell Rathbun for conversation, he confirmed that his congregation owes a great debt to the good will of First Baptist, where his congregation, House of Mercy, has been gathering and worshiping from its beginning in 1996.

At our meeting, Russell told the story of House of Mercy and its intentional engagement with the arts. The congregation was founded in the spring of 1996 with the express intention of offering a "blend of high church and low, of tradition and innovation, sincere worship and healthy skepticism." According to the statement that appears in their worship bulletin, the ministry offers "to create a New Church through the renewal of worship and theology among cynical Christians and the spiritually curious." Russell expanded the reality behind the mission statement. The ministry team is composed of Russell and two other ordained ministers, Mark Stenberg and Debbie Blue, and their musician, Chris Larson. When Russell and Chris were living in Seattle in the early 1990s, they observed with dismay that many of their friends did not go to church. This absence both puzzled and annoyed Russell and Chris, for they had affection for the church. They also wondered why was it that Good News for the world was so often seen as "bad news." Over a period of time Russell and Chris developed the notion that they would like to serve in a church where their friends might go. They moved to St. Paul in 1995; the following year they began their current ministry in a more or less organized way. Theirs is a ministry with the arts, so there is a touch of the theatrical about these early days, reminiscent of old Judy Garland and Mickey Rooney movies. It seems that Debbie Blue, a soulmate, was with them at the beginning as they faced their prospects. Together they developed a vision of what they wanted to do and said to themselves, "Let's start a church." They started House of Mercy.

Russell talked about those who attend this alternative congregation within the space of First Baptist. Though the ministry staff do not regard those who comprise the congregation as "members," the congregation supports about 350–375 folks overall. About 250 regularly attend at worship. They come from all over the area. Russell noted that the congregation consists largely of people in their 20s and 30s. He even spoke, wistfully I think, of trying to enlist some elderly people for balance! Though rooted in the Baptist tradition, his particular congregation draws, he says, from the larger Christian tradition. The people who are involved in the congregation's worship, small groups, and art programs are quite diverse and come from the whole spectrum of Protestant and Catholic persuasions; and many come from the realm of those with marginal and minimal Christian commitment.

Repeatedly Russell expressed gratitude to the Baptist church for space and support. As Baptists in the free church tradition, the ministry team feels they are expected to be entrepreneurs; that is, they must make their own way and do their own thing without much larger support or accountability. There is an increasing, and conflicting, awareness of wanting to be part of a larger historical church. But there was also the strong desire to remain independent. There was mention of the possible affiliation with the ELCA [Evangelical Lutheran Church in America]; but that is some time off, if at all.

House of Mercy is active in the St. Paul arts coalition and is part of the arts council. The signature of this congregation's life is its commitment to and involvement in the city's art world. By way of example, Russell mentioned the congregation's annual Stations of the Cross. In Lent, for the past three years, the congregation has invited 14 different artists "from all over the map" to create painting, sculpture, mixed media. On Monday in Holy Week the stations are installed in the church's sanctuary.

The church is then open throughout Holy Week with these artworks in place, and people are welcome and free to come and go as they wish. On Good Friday there is a procession, the Way of the Cross. The idea and the liturgical format are taken from the Roman Catholic service: readings, responses, hymns. The images are based on each traditional station and depict Christ's passion and crucifixion. Some of the works are literal; others are abstract. The service lasts about 35 minutes, with each stop along the way of the cross being about two or so minutes.

Russell next talked about one of the art shows House of Mercy had installed in the basement gallery area where we had our conversation. At one time the space may have been a cozy parish hall. Now it is a large cave-like room with white-washed stone walls – a flexible, open area easily converted, as needed, into gallery space, coffee house, or recital hall.

He referred to a *Confessional Show* involving five artists who were invited to create works about the Roman Catholic Confessional. Not for the first time was I struck by the singularity of a Baptist congregation invoking Roman Catholic traditions and practices. (We talked about this anomaly later at some length.) For now, Russell described the works in the *Confessional Show* as provocative: some were representational; others, mocking. He mentioned in particular a confessional booth with a broken handle so that no one could get in. Some interpreted the work as meaning the confessor was inaccessible; others observed that perhaps confession itself was impossible.

As we talked about specific art projects, Russell also referred to larger and more general issues. He underscored the congregation's deep commitment to living at the intersection of faith and culture in the city of St. Paul. Art, he noted, has the responsibility to open up eyes, and sometimes even shock, so that the gospel message can get through. The works in the exhibitions sponsored by House of Mercy challenge people to interact with religious themes and subject matter in the light of their current cultural situation.

Religious art, he reflected, is often bad, referring to what he called, "typical Sunday school illustrations." To illustrate his point about bad art in general and Sunday school art in particular Russell discussed a print show from the summer of 2001 called *The 20 Dollar Print Show*. It gathered works that indicate how religious imagery is appropriated by popular culture, in this case ill-conceived religious education illustrations. "It contained," he said, "many examples of Jesus jumping out at kids, bad stuff, confusing stuff."

One example he shared purportedly illustrated the "Love of God." Depicted was a narrow gate on the left marked HEAVEN, with a radiantly glowing Jesus gesturing a family of three along the road marked "Happiness." The road marker at the junction points to "The Love of God." Opposite Jesus is a vain, well-dressed couple in rich attire, self-indulgently observing themselves in a mirror. They stand alongside the road marked "Unhappiness."

Four signposts point down this road: "Love of Riches, Love of Pleasure, Love of Fame, Love of Power." It is, not surprisingly, a wider road with three wealthy folks running and leaping through the gate into the blazing fire beyond, the place clearly marked HELL. The print may be read as a very sanitized and culturally didactic reduction of Dante's *Divine Comedy*. Russell mentioned that examples of some of these works (along with much else) could be seen on their website: www.houseofmercy.org.

While the arts are a significant part of the ministry of House of Mercy, worship is central. Services take place on Sunday afternoons at 5:30. The order of worship is very important. Russell and his colleagues value the historical liturgy even though many creative paths are taken. The leaders see their worship service as a well-crafted weekly event in a style that might be described as "liturgical eclecticism." Taking what has worked in the Roman Catholic tradition, the Baptist tradition, and other Christian traditions, the congregation has borrowed and forged its own style.

Russell pointedly mentioned that the worship at House of Mercy deliberately steers a course away from "praise" services, which he feels do not attract the people which House of Mercy serves. Rather, the style of worship and the congregational singing lean toward country gospel music and poetry.

A band – actually more than one band each week – leads the assembly by playing white gospel music. There is often a guest artist, for the congregation values the artistic gifts of musicians in the community beyond their own assembly. "We acknowledge these gifts from God whether or not the artist does," Russell said.

The music sometimes is edgy, catching people by surprise, for there are many creative spikes – even occasional profanity – in the musical offerings. Still, the music and the preaching are for the sake of God's Word.

The ministerial staff, co-pastors, rotates leadership, based on the Roman Catholic Newman Center model.

On the Sunday I experienced worship at House of Mercy, I found the service to be precisely what Russell said it was – and more. The parking lot was full, the pews were fully occupied, and the communion service was fully eclectic. The Western rite was recognizably in place, though from the free church tradition. The informal, eclectic service was part stand-up repartee, part PBS pledge campaign, and part Prairie Home Companion. For all its diversity, the service had a Gospel center and was quite moving.

Liturgical objects, such as the thurible, Eucharist set and *candelium standus* were all commissioned by the congregation and crafted by Twin Cities artists, as noted in the bulletin. The *oblato recepticum* (from the pseudo-Latin for 'bread box') stood in front of the church, and people were asked to give their offerings if and when they chose – offering plates were not circulated. A smooth country music band and several guest artists led seasonal music ranging from "Silver Bells" to "O Come, All Ye Faithful."

The Reverend Debbie Blue took as her texts Isaiah 11 and Louise Erdrich's *The Last Report on the Miracles at Little No Horse*. She preached a provocative law-gospel sermon on God's judgment to the rapt crowd of mostly twenty-somethings. Her inviting manner of relating scripture and experience suggested some reasons that the congregation is called House of Mercy.

In our conversation, Russell noted that there are churches that know God emotionally, while other churches stress doctrine and intellect. House of Mercy attempts to maintain a balance, which it regards as an aesthetic way of knowing God. This approach is realized, naturally, in the emphasis on art. But is also comes about by developing an awareness of God's presence in small groups by actually being a traditional church. Not, Russell says, in the tradition of the 1950s; but rather in the manner of the 1650s.

It is clear that this reaching out and reaching back suggest what the congregation means when it defines itself as a blend of high and low, of tradition and innovation, sincere worship and healthy skepticism. "We feel we are developing a church our friends would go to, and a lot of our friends are artists. However, art is not used 'to reach people' so much as it is an expression for the love of God and for living out our life in faith."

In this regard Russell talked about the Louvin Gallery, a significant part of life at House of Mercy. The gallery is located in the basement of

First Baptist Church. Its name derives from Ira (1924–1965) and Charlie (b. 1927) Louvin, country gospel singers. The gallery is home to music as well as art. One of the missions of the gallery is to preserve, and encourage people to discover, old and new church music. Many people, Russell observed, want to hear and sing the old stuff, not just the sounds currently in the culture. We "want to reach young people and not throw out the hymnal. Like the Louvin brothers, we want to sink into the tradition."

Over two years ago Charlie, the surviving brother, organized bands to do music at House of Mercy, bands with names like The Carpetbaggers, Urban Hillbilly Quartet, Lackluster Dodge, Angel and many more. This signal concert, which took place September 29 and 30, 2001, affirmed that "Nobody's all Saturday night. Nobody's all Sunday morning." The gallery, which now is used for music, paintings, sculpture, and other works of art, is named after the Brothers Louvin. In addition to the musical programs, the gallery mounts five or six shows a year. I visited the opening of one show ten days before Christmas, and I found the cave-like gallery transformed into a series of intimate spaces by art and hanging fabric panels. The exhibit, consisting of three figural paintings and three constructions, was modest by museum or large gallery standards. Yet, the several people who were there in the hour I spent stayed to look deeply. One or two spent a great deal of time looking at and pondering the works of art hanging there.

My conversation with Russell also touched on House of Mercy's Artbus. This is a mobile art machine, a '72 VW bus with easels affixed to the sides. The canvases are good and the paint materials are high quality. In warm weather a driver takes the bus around the city and periodically stops to ask people on the street to paint on one of these canvases. "After all God is creator," Russell observed, "and God's people should be offered the chance to create – even though relatively few do."

Toward the end of our time together, Russell and I talked about the congregation's print studio, called Mercy Press. Monica Larson, a congregational supporter and a printmaker, has developed her handmade art on behalf of the congregation. "It is definitely not slick," Russell mused. Her work illustrates the flyers for the Louvin Gallery. Christmas cards and even the cover for a CD come from the press. Russell showed me the small recording studio in the back where CDs are burned with local bands that happen to go to church here. The print shop, the recordings, the homegrown and community-based art efforts are all part of what Russell calls the "do-it-yourself aesthetic."

In parting, Russell mused that any congregation should be doing evangelism and proclaiming the Good News. In performing their ministry, "House of Mercy is careful not to use people or use them up. We need to proclaim faith not shame people."

Russell and his colleagues are content to be about the business of trying to create a New Church through the renewal of worship and theology among cynical Christians, the spiritually curious, and minds open to the arts.

At one point in their life together the three pastors tried to capture what it was that motivated them in their work. The result was a mission statement which reads: "The mission and vision of House of Mercy is to grow a church through the recovery of grace-based theology, the practice of liturgical eclecticism, and active service in the world." That vision may have been the reason *City Pages* recognized House of Mercy as "Best of the Twin Cities 2000 – Best church for the non-churchgoing."

About the author

Robert Brusic is Seminary Pastor emeritus at Luther Seminary in St. Paul, Minnesota. He has nurtured a lifelong love of the fine arts through course work, reading, and frequent museum attendance. He is the author of *And Grace Will Lead Me Home: The Jerry Evenrud Collection of Images of the Parable of the Prodigal Son* (Minneapolis: Lutheran University Press, 2007). He has also written for *Word and World, Lectionary Homiletics, and ARTS.*

Singing in the Wilderness
Music, Art and Life at saint benedict's table

Jamie Howison

In much of his written work, and perhaps most notably in an essay entitled "Rethinking Church Models through Scripture,"[1] the Old Testament scholar Walter Brueggemann has argued persuasively that as was the case for Israel in exile, the key task for an increasingly marginalized church is that of re-texting the community in its foundational – and often subversive – narratives. I actually wonder to what degree we have really faced our current reality of marginalization. To borrow another image from Brueggemann, the church has been moved from judge's bench to witness stand, where we've found that we are but one in a whole series of others, all waiting to give witness in an increasingly pluralistic society.[2]

The truth is that the church is no longer a key societal arbiter of what is right or true or good, but one of the many voices asking to be heard. We are in a situation analogous to Israel in exile – though our move into exile has not been marked by that level of violence and upheaval – wherein our language and our practices are not echoed, carried or supported by the broader culture; or certainly not in any significant way.

This business of re-texting is crucial work; yet do we invite our artists, our singers, our poets, to immerse us in our own narratives in such a way that we might hear them, and see them, and know them anew? Do we call on these folks to undo us, break our hearts, and help us see with fresh eyes? Or do we insist instead that they *behave*, and give us only that which reinforces all we think we already know? Why has Thomas Kinkade, with his paintings of quaint cottages and lighthouses, been deemed the artist of choice in North American evangelical subculture, and even christened the "painter of light"? He may paint a nice little lighthouse, but it has nothing on a piece like van Gogh's "Starry Night"; a painting which seems to actually project its own light. And what about what is sometimes called the "J-factor" in the Christian pop music scene? That is the number of times an artist uses the name of Jesus in a song, and it is actually one of the things that the industry has traditionally looked for when it programs for radio, with an adequate number of invocations of the name of Jesus increasing a song's viability in that particular market.

It is possible, of course, to come up with examples of material that doesn't fit here: the music of Bruce Cockburn or Sufjan Stevens, the novels of Graham Greene or Frederick Buechner, the poetry of T. S. Eliot or Lucy Shaw; and thank goodness there are such examples... but the fact is, this is the cluster of artists and writers who almost always leap to mind. They are a distinct minority.

And again, how could we possibly think it wise to attempt to shape a Christian church without reference to the poetic and artistic imagination? Without telling – and telling it in all of its oddness – the story that in fact shapes us? Not a partial, tidied up, edges-sanded-off polite version of the story, but the whole works.

Calvin Seerveld, a scholar in the field of philosophical aesthetics, writes:
> What really has given "christian art" its bad name has been the cheap way that stock motifs such as conversions, happy endings or Bible phrases are popped in like vitamin pills to pep up one-dimensional, outdated material which is then sold as "Christian novels," "Christian plays," or "Christian songs." Using Christ in that way is, in my judgment, taking his Name in vain. You do not get the rare pearl of Christian art by dubbing in a few crosses or chalices, or by draping a good-old-days kind of atmosphere around a trite plot. Christian art in our days, I believe, will take suffering to produce.[3]

It will take suffering to produce? Suffering? Who is going to sign up for that? Yet for the artist who is a Christian, maybe it is not so much a case of signing on as it is being simply prepared to do one's art *authentically*. When, for instance, a major record company suggested to the singer/songwriter Steve Bell that that he would be more marketable if he didn't sing all of those psalms, he basically had to confront the fact that psalms are what he does; to trim the faith out of his music would be to truncate himself, both as a person and as an artist.

In the words of Walter Brueggemann,
> ... an alternative world is possible. The old world is not a given; it is a fraud. Another world is possible – in our imaginations: we listen and imagine differently. In our liberation we entertain different realities not yet given in hardware, so far only very soft ware, carried only

by narrative and song and poem and oracle (and I would add, by painting and sculpture and dance and, and, and...) said before being embodied, but said and we listen. As we listen we push out to the possibility and are held by it like a visioning child with a dream.[4]

And from imagination comes practice; not just personal practice, but communal, public practice which from time to time actually manages to do something real and lasting.

I'd push Brueggemann, though, on his image of the "visioning child with a dream," because sometimes the re-texting – our re-immersion in the narratives which give us our shape – which our poets and painters offer is more like a nightmare, or at least a forceful wake-up call. To draw on the insight of the songwriter Bruce Cockburn, we need our poets to teach us new ways to see, and that isn't always a pretty or comfortable thing.[5]

So why, then, do we keep using the arts for little more than glorified sermon illustrations? Music as the emotional tag that gets us opened up for the preacher?

Is it possible to create the kind of Christian communities wherein the poets are listened to, nurtured, and supported? In real ways? What might it look like to take seriously the church's marginalized status, and to begin to rise to the same challenge which faced Israel in its exile in Babylon: that of re-texting the community? Re-texting *our* communities, and not only with the preached word – which is something as a preacher I'm pretty committed to – but also the word painted, sculpted, sung, chanted, filmed, danced, performed and offered in every way imaginable... literally imaginable! Most churches, including my own, have a full-time preacher and a part-time musician, but why don't we have a poet or a painter on our staff? A writer-in-residence? A film-maker? A director? A choreographer?

In this Christian vision, suggests Seerveld,

> ...art and literature as human activity is not simply a harmless pleasurable emotion or a cultured response to unconscious drives which is the artist's own business: this vision takes art and literature and brings it firmly into the presence of God and an earthshaking drama where angels peer expectantly over the human shoulders to see what is coming out of the palette or typewriter."[6]

And the angels peer expectantly because they know how deeply we need to be re-immersed in our foundational story; how badly we need to be fundamentally and imaginatively re-texted; how powerfully we need to relearn how to sing the Lord's song in this increasingly strange land.

Admittedly, our community of saint benedict's table hasn't yet taken the step of freeing the resources for a resident artist or poet, but we do try to make room for the artists among us to share their various visions. We have twice now held unjuried weekend long art exhibits, celebrating the visual artists of our community. On both occasions we rented gallery space in our city's arts district, and opened the exhibits with prayers of blessing and wine and cheese receptions. On both occasions close to 20 people contributed pieces, ranging from photography and painting to sculpture and installations. We look forward to mounting another such exhibit, though we are determined to do so only as the desire arises from our circle of artists. To get caught in the trap of having to do something annually simply because we've done it twice before...that is a trap to avoid.

We have also incorporated the gifts of several of our visual artists into our liturgical life. Helen Lyons has donated a set of prints of her original *Stations of the Cross*, as well as pieces of pottery for use as communion vessels; Lola Eidse has gifted us with a series of hand-lettered and illuminated seasonal "liturgy cards," which are colour photocopied and distributed as our basic "prayer book." Others have loaned us pieces of art to be used for a Sunday or for a season, and these serve (along with our more conventional icons) as points of visual focus in the liturgy.

Drama is something that we have not yet really explored, though given that we include in our community several people with at least some theatre background, there is some interest in at least exploring our options. We do not, however, imagine that this would take place as a part of our regular Sunday liturgy; a liturgy, incidentally, that we would understand to be, among other things, a drama offered to the glory of God by the whole gathered community. There has been some discussion with Calvin Seerveld about mounting a production of his *The Greatest Song: in critique of Solomon*, which is a dramatized and sung re-reading of the Song of Songs. Again, were we to mount this work – and Dr. Seerveld is hopeful that we will – it would not be as a sermon-aid or as a piece of didactic drama, but as a work of theatre to be shared in the context of our city's arts scene.

The one area in which we have taken significant steps is that of music, specifically music for worship. We do have a staff musician, a journeyman bass guitar player named Larry Campbell, who is paid a stipend for what is, at least in theory, a one day a week position. Rather than serving as the typical worship music *leader*, the staff musician's role is to coordinate, support, and mentor the musicians of the community; it is, in a real sense, very much both pastoral and liturgical in scope. With Larry's support and guidance, there are currently five different ensembles on the roster for worship leadership (only one of which he actually leads), and each is given all but complete free rein in the choice, development, and even writing of music for the liturgy. I say "all but free rein," in that each works within the boundaries of the liturgical calendar and the lectionary, and all are shaped by the ongoing question of how their music aids this community in its life of worship.

To fully understand how this latter question really informs all that we do in our liturgy, it is important to have a picture of how our space is configured for worship. At no time do the musicians play to the congregation; their role is always to play with. Our community shares space in All Saints Church in Winnipeg, an 80-year-old building of neo-Gothic design, configured with a high altar, chancel and rood screen, and fixed pews seating 450. A few rows of pews have been removed from the front, giving us enough room to lead worship from the area at the foot of the chancel steps. We use a small carved oak table as our altar, and our musicians play seated off to the side, oriented with the community toward the table. They are amplified, but only to enhance their ability to lead the community in its worship. It would be considered a problem if the music was so loud that people in the general congregation found it hard to sing.

Having unleashed and freed our musicians to explore writing new music for use in the liturgy, we have been almost overwhelmed by what has been produced. In fact, within the first year of our formal establishment as a congregation, in the autumn of 2004, we were in the planning stages for the production of a CD of original music, which was released as *We Will Not Be Silent* in January 2007. This seems to have led to a kind of consolidation of our musical vision, in that several of our writers have become increasingly comfortable in exploring their various musical voices; new music is produced in response to the seasons and readings on a regular basis, and we've now built up a pretty solid repertoire of material specifically written for our context. One of our truly inspired and inspiring writers, Jenny Moore-Koslowsky, has produced an "extended play" single CD entitled *Songs for listening to on the train with an excellent set of headphones and an ambivalent heart.*

In many respects, it is the freeing of the musicians to find and express their voices in and for the community that has created such a creative environment. That "freeing up" is deep and thorough; it invites the musicians and writers to help us to find the voice to say what we need to say, but have not yet found the words or the melody to do so with. We know they are there, but we need the singer – the poet – to first give them voice.

Witness this reflection from Jenny Moore-Koslowsky:

> *I go to saint benedict's table because I do not have to have faith to participate in faithfulness. I attend because someone reads scripture for me, because someone prays on my behalf, because someone else makes the meal. I have often felt like it is insane that I offer music, or ideas, to such a monumental liturgy, but I don't feel as though I make the words, or form the songs. You make the songs, we each bring the music, I just ask you to sing it out with me – to sing what is already in us, what we have already discovered, survived, kept hidden and become. It has been a privilege to write songs for a community that never denies their own weakness, never gets enchanted by their own thoughts, and never gives a damn how many people show up.*

One or two of our initiatives might turn out to be good ideas for other church communities to adapt to their own contexts, and if that is the case then more power to you. More to the point, though, I am convinced that every church in every community across the continent will sooner or later need to take seriously the place of imagination in reconstituting themselves as a re-texted, and thus story-formed, people.

This is the singing of the Lord's song in a strange land, in a language both old and new. But without the willingness to try – again – to give voice – again – we are caught in the same despair as Israel courted in Babylon as its poets hung up their harps and vowed themselves to silence in face of the chaos of exile.

But can we do other than to try to make space for such voices? From Amos Wilder's *Theopoetic*: "When imagination fails doctrines become ossified, witness and proclamation wooden, doxologies and litanies empty, consolations hollow, and ethics legalistic."[7]

Can any of our communities afford not to learn to sing the Lord's song in new and imaginative ways in this increasingly strange land?

About the author

Jamie Howison is a priest of the Anglican Church and the founding pastor of saint benedict's table, a missional congregation of the Diocese of Rupert's Land in Winnipeg. A graduate of the University of Winnipeg and of Trinity College, Toronto, he serves as a member of the Primate's Theological Commission of the Anglican Church of Canada. Throughout his twenty years of ordained ministry, he has understood writing to be an important part of his priestly vocation, and has contributed to a variety of publications including *Sojourners*, *The Anglican Journal*, *Esprit* and *Canada Lutheran*, as well as to the collection *Get Up Off Your Knees: preaching the U2 catalogue* published by Cowley Publications. This article incorporates material from an address delivered at *Telling the Truth '07: a conference on the arts and the worshipping church*, held in the fall of 2007 in Victoria, British Columbia.

1   WALTER BRUEGGEMANN, "RETHINKING CHURCH MODELS THROUGH SCRIPTURE," *CADENCES OF HOME* (LOUISVILLE, KY: WESTMINSTER JOHN KNOX PRESS, 1997), PP. 99-109.
2   BRUEGGEMANN, "LIFE-OR-DEATH, DE-PRIVILEGED COMMUNICATION," *DEEP MEMORY, EXUBERANT HOPE* (MINNEAPOLIS: FORTRESS PRESS, 2000), PP. 20-21.
3   CALVIN SEERVELD, *BEARING FRESH OLIVE LEAVES* (TORONTO: TORONTO TUPPENCE PRESS, 2000), P. 17.
4   WALTER BRUEGGEMANN, "PREACHING AS SUBVERSION," *DEEP MEMORY, EXUBERANT HOPE* (MINNEAPOLIS: FORTRESS PRESS, 2000), P. 17.
5   BRUCE COCKBURN, "MAYBE THE POET," *STEALING FIRE*, TRUE NORTH RECORDS 1984.
6   SEERVELD, *A CHRISTIAN CRITIQUE OF ART AND LITERATURE* (TORONTO: TUPPENCE PRESS, 1995), P. 16.
7   AMOS NIVEN WILDER, *THEOPOETIC* (LIMA, OHIO: ACADEMIC RENEWAL PRESS), P. 2.

Embracing the Arts
Reflecting God's Grace
Keri K. Wehlander

© Ruth Irving

If you read through Glebe-St. James United Church's Mission Statement, one line is certain to catch your attention:

> *God is calling us in love to reflect God's grace...in our embrace of the arts to seek God and enrich human life...*

So, how, exactly, does this congregation in Ottawa, Ontario, fulfill this part of their Mission Statement?

Concerts, musicals, choirs, and classes on visual arts and drama all are a part of the ongoing life of this congregation. A particular emphasis is placed on children in the arts programming. Janet Guillen Nield, in her role as Christian Education Staff Associate, makes sure that the mid-week visual art, drama, and music programs, Sunday school, Sunday morning worship, and summer programs for children are all integrated in a holistic manner.

The "Arts Under One Roof" program came to Glebe-St. James in 2002, when the congregation hired Janet Guillen Nield. She initiated the program, and describes it in this way:

> The vision of the program is to provide the opportunity for spiritual growth for children and youth through art, music, and drama. The program was set up when the congregation realized that children have many demands on their time. Spiritual formation...can be done at a variety of times during the week – not just Sunday morning. As well, "Arts Under One Roof" is a way that the congregation reaches out to the whole community week after week.

Visual art, drama, and music classes are offered after school, as well as on Saturdays, and are taught by professional teachers. "Arts Under One Roof" also offers arts-oriented day camps in the summer. Any child in the community can take part, as all of these classes are "non-denominational." The church even has an "art room" – a room set up specifically for all those creating visual art in these classes.

One of the program's teachers, Lisa Thomas, reflects on her role in the program in this way:

> I see my purpose as art facilitator as someone who sees all children as equal. I want to help each child explore their inner space – with the idea that this will make them more connected to what is really important in themselves. I feel especially rewarded when a child comes to me, barely able to make a mark on the paper from fear of not being good enough or being judged, and after a few months or even weeks is able to succumb to the joy of his or her own flow of expression. Often, I am completely enraptured by a little scribble of a 5-year-old, or a wild and vibrant wash of colour of a 9-year-old, and I feel inspired and even in awe of their innate understanding of composition and order and chaos and feeling.

Through the "Arts Under One Roof" program, three choirs for children and youth are also offered. These choirs take part in worship, congregational musicals, and special events for local churches.

Alex Totten-Thomas is an eight-year-old who takes part in both the visual art classes and the choir through "Arts Under One Roof." When asked about the program, Alex responds, "I really like it because you get to do fun stuff." He also indicates that working with the pastels is one of his favourite things to do.

Alex is the son of Ron Totten and Gord Thomas, a same-gender couple. They wanted to make sure that Alex would have a positive environment to explore art in. Alex lives with ADHD, and is a very active child.

Ron comments that these programs are "a perfect match for Alex." He appreciates the supportive approach that the instructors offer, and feels that "it is important that there is a spiritual component" in this program. He stresses that this spiritual element is not "in your face," which he appreciates.

Another reason that this program has been important is that Ron and Gord were told when they adopted Alex that his birth mother was artistic. It has been important for them to offer this opportunity to Alex, as well as helping him to have this place of connection with his birth mother.

The program has opened up a number of possibilities for Alex. Ron has found that they have had some important conversations as a result of the artwork that Alex has brought home. Ron also observes that, "Going to choir and art class creates a domino effect in terms of the wider church community. Alex knows everybody. The art programs enlarge his world, and make church fun."

The Sunday school program also has a strong arts component, and incorporates a storytelling emphasis. Following the encounter with the story, children are free to explore different and usually non-directed responses to the story through various art media.

Glebe-St. James has also experimented with offering "Monday School" – a Sunday school class offered on Mondays that intentionally joins Christian spirituality with art education for children in grades 3–6.

Music is an important part of the life of the congregation. A senior choir meets once a week to practice for their participation in worship. They take part in local music festivals, and, on occasion, give concerts. Soloists and instrumentalists are often part of the Sunday liturgy.

There is also a Sunday afternoon concert series, which offers a wide variety of events, ranging from a lecture-recital on the life and songs of Cole Porter to an organ concert featuring works by Buxtehude and Bach.

The congregation has had a tradition of putting on a musical once a year. Although there has been a bit of a hiatus in this program, plans are in the works to reestablish it. Some of the musicals they have performed in the past include: *100% Chance of Rain; The Trouble of Zerubbabel; The Puzzling Parables*; and *Jonah and the Whale*. All ages take part, but there is a strong emphasis on the musicals being child friendly, so that as many children as possible can participate.

Randa Zeitoun and her family have enjoyed taking part in many of the musicals at the church. She observes that her children end up

> singing these songs from the musicals in the summertime at the cottage around the campfire. The music is beautiful, and it proves they liked what they sang. They are also remembering what it means – something from the Bible has touched them and stayed with them.

Even Christine Johnson, one of the ordained ministers in the congregation, brings a background in the arts to the congregation. She worked for six years as an arts administrator and artistic director in an art gallery prior to studying theology. As a part of her doctoral thesis, she studied acting and applied this experience to her studies of the art of preaching. She is also a quilt and fibre artist.

In reflecting on the relationship between arts and faith, Johnson has this to say:

> The arts have long been part of the Christian tradition. They express our deepest desires to create, desires which I believe come from God. When we're able to intentionally name the arts as a specific way that we worship and honour God, it opens the entire congregation to all kinds of possibilities. The arts open and draw us into the spirit of inspiration and experimentation. They show us an alternative way of being that often leads us to seeking justice for all. When we name and claim the arts as part of our spiritual practice, they become another way to experience God.

At Glebe-St. James, the commitment to embrace the arts as part of their spiritual practice and mission is evident. As a result, "the spirit of inspiration and experimentation" that Johnson speaks of is alive and well.

About the author

Keri K. Wehlander (<u>www.creativeworship.ca</u>) is an author, hymn lyricist, and retreat leader. She is the series editor for *Experience! Faith Formation Curriculum for Adults* (Wood Lake Publishing Inc.) and the author of *Circles of Grace: Worship and Prayer in the Everyday* (United Church Publishing House). Her writings have been included in various anthologies in both North America and Europe. Keri is the editor of *Creating Change: The Arts as Catalyst for Spiritual Transformation*.

Back to the Future
Fourth-Century Style Reaches Bay Area Seekers

Trudy Bush

© David Sanger / www.davidsanger.com

A half hour before the Sunday morning service begins, St. Gregory of Nyssa Episcopal Church in San Francisco already displays the holy chaos that characterizes its worship. In the domed entrance hall a choir is practicing motets. In the rectangular "synagogue" area, where worshipers' chairs face each other across a long raised platform, the liturgist is rehearsing readers for the service. Worship leaders in brightly colored Liberian vestments hand out spiral-bound songbooks and welcome newcomers.

Visitors are sure to be struck by the visual power of the scene as well. Circling the dome above the altar are vivid representations of saints, not all of them Christian. Gandhi, Malcolm X, Abraham Joshua Heschel, the Buddha and Muhammad are among the figures who form the two-tier line dance, along with Fyodor Dostoevsky and Ella Fitzgerald, Isaiah, Julian of Norwich, Martin Luther, Elizabeth I and Iqbal Hasih, a Pakistani murdered at age 13 for speaking out against child labor. Above the saints, who were painted by Mark Dukes, is a text from St. Gregory: "The one thing truly worthwhile . . . is becoming God's friend."

On one wall, below the icon of a dancing Christ, is a framed rubbing of a tablet from a seventh-century Eastern, or Nestorian, church in western China. On the opposite wall, at the entrance to the synagogue area, the lectern is draped in African cloth and surrounded by Ethiopian ceremonial standards. Above the preacher's seat, which is a wide howdab from Thailand (a canopied seat for riding on an elephant), is a floor-to-ceiling icon depicting the marriage of the soul with Christ.

At ten o'clock, music director Sanford Dole calls everyone to gather around the altar and announces that the service will be sung a cappella. "Sing the melody in unison during the first stanza," he instructs, "then break into parts for the rest of each hymn or chant." He leads the congregation in rehearsing two verses of each selection.

Then comes the biggest surprise for newcomers. The leaders demonstrate the steps of a line-dance that worshipers will use to process to their seats. Everyone practices the step. Then, books opened to the processional hymn, the singing and dancing congregation follows the candle, the cross, the rector, worship leaders carrying colorful ceremonial umbrellas, and choir members beating tambourines, ringing bells and clanging cymbals until everyone finds a seat.

Worship then settles into a more expected pattern. Each reading is followed by the tones of solemn Asian gongs and ample silence for reflection. The rector, seated like a rabbi in a first-century synagogue, preaches on the texts. Then another surprise: the rector invites worshipers to share a personal experience that illustrates the theme of the sermon. Several people do. It becomes clear why members of the congregation sit facing each other – so they can easily engage each other in the storytelling and the bidding prayers that follow.

After the service of the word it is time to move to the table to share bread and wine. The music director teaches another dance step. Singing a hymn, people move to the altar, right hand on the shoulder of the person in front, left hand holding the song book – right foot forward, left behind, right forward, kick left, kick right, right forward again – until all the verses are sung. Encircling the altar and the host, worshipers sing and chant the Great Thanksgiving. Leaders offer the bread and wine and the choir sings.

After a final hymn and blessing, worship moves seamlessly into fellowship. The altar becomes the serving table for coffee and juice. Carts of pastries and bread appear beneath the Christ icon. Visitors are invited to tour and learn more about St. Gregory's. People in need of prayer are invited to come forward for anointing and spiritual support. Over the next half hour the crowd gradually thins.

Most of the people who join St. Gregory's have not belonged to or attended any church for three years or more. Many have had no church experience at all. Most have no denominational affiliation. The average age of the adults in the congregation is between 34 and 45 – which is 20 years younger than the average Episcopal congregation. About half of St. Gregory's members are families; the other half singles, gay and straight.

Those who pass through St. Gregory's welcoming doors on Sunday mornings come from the same group targeted by "seeker" churches: the growing number of people who report that they have no religious affiliation at all. In the San Francisco Bay Area and parts of the Pacific Northwest, that number is 90 percent of the population, according to the latest census. This means that among the people who gather to worship on Sunday morning some would call themselves Christian, but others might invoke some other faith or spirituality, and many would have no allegiance to any tradition.

In serving this eclectic mix of worshipers, say rectors Donald Schell and Richard Fabian, St. Gregory's is like a church of the fourth century – the era of St. Gregory of Nyssa. As Christianity became the newly adopted faith of the Roman Empire, the rectors note, the church attracted faithful Christians, curious pagans, adherents of various schools of philosophy, devotees of mystery religions, and many who came only because their social position encouraged it.

In fact, John Baldwin, a professor at Weston Theological Seminary, said after visiting St. Gregory's: "I have just had the closest possible experience of what worship was like in the fourth century." A visitor from Africa commented: "The church service here is the closest thing I've experienced in America to a village worship service in Africa."

For Fabian and Schell, however, St. Gregory is designed with American seekers in mind. But whereas most seeker churches work with the models of the shopping mall and the television audience in designing their space and worship service, Fabian likens worship at St. Gregory's to a rock concert, which he calls the modern secular experience that most closely resembles the divine liturgy. He seeks a worship that is an intense participatory experience of movement, singing, dancing and bonding. Schell adds another analogy: "We also follow the model of a dinner party in how we welcome people. We ask, 'How can we invite people in?'"

"We want the people who come to St. Gregory's to sense that they're part of a worldwide culture and a worldwide religion," Fabian says. "That's the way the Bay Area is – it has great diversity. Many people choose to live in California for the kind of life they can have together here. They would be more affluent if they lived elsewhere, but they want to be here…"

Schell tells of growing up in sermon-centered evangelical services, which left him feeling dissatisfied and spiritually hungry. "Even when I was only 12 or 13 years old, I had the sense that there was more we could be doing together at worship to bring us closer to the sense of mystery, to move us. There could be more beauty and challenge." That sense led him on the quest that has culminated in St. Gregory's.

"There's a great opportunity now for doing powerful, participatory worship," Fabian says. "People love it. We do this because it's a powerful spiritual, emotional and experiential resource." Schell adds, "Over 30 years as a priest I've seen what can happen for people who are gathered together and making something holy of whatever anyone present has to offer. I've seen how transforming it is for people's lives and how it opens them to an experience of God." Worship of this kind "takes people who are first touched in a human or an aesthetic way and moves them toward genuine religious conversion, to a passion for God, a love of Jesus."

In describing their conception of worship, Schell and Fabian point to the example of Jesus and the practice of the early church. Jesus brought a community into being by feasting with strangers and sinners, actions that served "to inaugurate and enact God's work of welcoming all, pouring the Spirit out on all flesh." Following that example, St. Gregory's invites all to join in the Eucharistic feast, to participate actively in worship, and to worship in a space that includes folk art from many traditions.

In its approach to building community, the congregation is again doing something different from most seeker churches, even if the goal is similar, the rectors say. "My impression is that seeker churches build community because they think people need it," Schell says. "We think that the building of community around Jesus' table is our central calling. The first [approach] is at a certain level the same kind of thinking that says we need to have surplus parking. 'Community' can simply be fit into a checklist of what people are looking for."

By contrast, he says, Jesus created community for its transforming power, "calling people out of their loneliness, isolation and alienation and into communion – both in the literal sense of the community of the table and in the extended sense of communion, fellowship, friendship, mutual support and the challenge to work together."

Fabian adds that the seeker churches with which he's familiar do invite people to get involved, but they don't do it through the liturgy. "It's an issue of design. Do you design the participation to be during the liturgy, or do you design it to be in other places in small groups, for instance." One reason St. Gregory's does it through the liturgy is because that was the practice of the early church. "What we call traditional worship was originally highly participatory, and it's been hugely popular through the centuries. It is the foundation for all liturgical traditions."

As the name of the church suggests, worship at St. Gregory's is heavily influenced by traditions of Eastern Orthodoxy. The Orthodox Church, Schell says, "offers a 2,000-year history of popular liturgy in the vernacular. And early on, in the fourth through the sixth centuries, it was also a church dealing with large popular gatherings of half-converted people. It's a good model for today's situation of people wandering into the church with open minds but without being sure what they believe or why." Fabian and Schell also find in the Orthodox tradition a spiritual and aesthetic element to which they resonate, and they have drawn on the material it offers – visually, musically and liturgically.

But the congregation is firmly Episcopal, happy to be a contributing partner of the Episcopal Diocese of California. It is Orthodox in the sense of believing that the liturgical tradition of the Eastern Church belongs to all Christianity. "It's part of the Christian storehouse of treasures," Fabian says.

The church's worship practices, says Schell, "are aimed at taking people out of the constraints of having to be a certain way in church. They move people into a much more spontaneous, direct, immediate engagement with each other and with the word and sacrament." Paradoxically, spontaneity requires careful preparation. "To create a setting in which people feel safe enough to speak, dance and share in the sermon one needs a very well-rehearsed vehicle. Only then will people feel secure enough to try something new."

Dance is incorporated into the service because "dancing is one of the most profound and ancient parts of worship. Its association with Jesus didn't vanish until the 19th century." The rectors admit that people new to the church aren't always comfortable with the dancing, but they feel that it's important to "push people's comfort level at church in the way that anything exciting and creative does. We don't say to people, 'Do this if it's comfortable.' We simply invite. Staying comfortable doesn't push people into new territory." They are convinced, as Fabian puts it, that "movement, touching and breathing together create a more complex, profound community. The things that we do together are the most profound way of changing who we are."

Fabian and Schell began envisioning a church like St. Gregory's while both were chaplains at Yale University in the 1970s. Fabian's family wealth enabled them to set up a foundation, All Saints Company, that would seek and provide funding for the church they imagined. St. Gregory's came into existence in 1978 as an experiment in the renewal of liturgical and parish life. Fabian and Schell's dream came to full fruition 20 years later when, after years of sharing space in other church buildings, the congregation moved to its own new structure in the Prothero Hill area, a light-industrial section of the city.

A micro-brewery stands across the street from the church on one side, a teddy-bear factory on the other. By Midwestern standards, both the lot and the church are small, but in San Francisco's inflated housing market the church was almost prohibitively expensive. Only a $1 million gift from Fabian's family enabled the congregation to complete the project. But once in its own spacious quarters, the congregation quickly grew, doubling in the first few months and doubling again in the following three years.

The building is built in the style of Siberian Orthodox churches, mixed with some elements of Japanese fortress architecture. The design began with a floor plan Schell and Fabian had in mind from early on – a plan taken from pre-fifth-century Syrian synagogues at a time when Christians and Jews used similar buildings. The Syrian synagogues provided space "defined not by a sacralized event, but by the gathering and shaping of a fluid community of people," Schell says. St. Gregory's floor plan began with two architectural principles: that "what the Christian community does when it gathers creates and contains its holy space," and that "architectural spaces for Christian community will support welcoming and belonging and giving and receiving of grace-filled gifts."

To show how this kind of space helps break down barriers and to welcome people, Schell tells the story of a parishioner who wanted to share with the hungry the blessing she felt when first welcomed to the altar table. Her response led eventually to a food pantry that is located around the table. The program gives away bags of groceries to the poor every Friday and has enrolled a hundred volunteers. "Each week our congregation of neighbors and friends who need groceries is as big as our combined Sunday liturgical gatherings. Some who first came to us for groceries now are attending liturgy and have become members." The holy table around which the congregation gathers to share the sacred meal shapes a Eucharistically inspired ministry.

St. Gregory's has a large staff for a moderate-sized congregation. But only the two rectors serve full-time. The music director, assisting presbyter, director of pastoral care, director of family and children's ministries, parish administrator, event coordinator and executive director of the All Saints Company (the foundation supporting the church) are all part-timers. Talented volunteers also bring their expertise to the congregation, producing St. Gregory's videotapes and designing and maintaining its exceptional Web site (www.saintgregorys.org).

Does something distinctly Christian emerge from St. Gregory's open and religiously diverse congregation? Without creedal consensus, can one build a community patterned on Jesus' community of disciples? The rectors and the congregation struggle with these questions. They are trying, Schell wrote recently, to find "a way to be truly christian that does not exclude, condemn or marginalize experiences that are not christian." (Schell says he uses the small "c" for "christian" to suggest that "we don't mean to claim exclusive right to that identity.")

Fabian sees Christian identity emerging as part of a conversation that God is carrying on with humanity – a conversation that we don't define, limit or direct. "What we have seen in Jesus allows us to recognize what God is doing everywhere," he says. "The whole plan is shown clearly in Jesus, and it's a plan for the whole world."

According to Schell, the congregation is trying to meet and embrace Jesus while also embodying Gregory of Nyssa's discovery: "By the grace of God, all humanity is already one." The church patterns its preaching and practice on Jesus' teaching and its sacramental practice on his ministry. Instead of focusing on each person's individual faith, the congregation tries to imitate what Jesus did. Instead of asking people to assent to a particular set of beliefs, the community listens to all the ways in which its people perceive Jesus.

"Among our many voices, some skeptical, some deeply committed to Jesus the teacher, some mystical..., one faith emerges," Schell said. "That faith lives in the chorus of our many questions, intuitions, experiences and simple certainties, our sorrows and joys, our compassion and love and desire to serve others. Something whole emerges from the many different ways we hold Jesus." Fabian sums up the ministry this way: "What makes us Christian is all that we do together. The people are participating in the great acts of worship, and that participation is what makes them Christian..."

St. Gregory's highly participatory worship may not be for everyone, but it would be hard not to be moved by this congregation's way of continuing the long conversation God has had with humanity.

About the author

Trudy Bush has served as an associate editor for *Christian Century* for 15 years. Prior to that, she taught English at the University of Wisconsin – Whitewater. She has a Ph.D. in English, with a specialty in Victorian literature.

Bibliography

Adams, Doug, and Diane Apostolos-Cappadona, eds. *Dance As Religious Studies*. New York: The Crossroad Publishing Company, 1990

Adams, Doug, and Michael E. Moynahan eds. *Postmodern Worship and the Arts*. San Jose: Resource Publications, 2002

Apostolos-Cappadona, Diane, ed. *Art, Creativity, and the Sacred*. New York: The Crossroad Publishing Company, 1984

Azara, Nancy. *Spirit Taking Form: Making a Spiritual Practice of Making Art*. Boston: Red Wheel, 2002

Bell, John. *The Singing Thing: A Case for Congregational Song*. Chicago: GIA, 2000

Buckley, Ray. *Dancing with Words: Storytelling as Legacy, Culture, and Faith*. Nashville: Discipleship Resources, 2004

Butler Bass, Diana. *Christianity for the Rest of Us: How the Neighborhood Church Is Transforming the Faith*. New York: HarperCollins Publishers, 2006

Butler Bass, Diana and Joseph Stewart-Sicking, eds. *From Nomads to Pilgrims: Stories from Practicing Congregations*. Herndon: Alban Institute Inc., 2006

Chinn, Nancy. *Spaces for Spirit: Adorning the Church*. Chicago: Liturgy Training Publications, 1998

Coupar, Regina. *The Art of Soul: An Artist's Guide to Spirituality*. Ottawa: Novalis, 2002

Degler, Teri. *The Fiery Muse: Creativity and The Spiritual Quest*. Toronto: Random House Canada, 1996

Diaz, Adriana. *Freeing the Creative Spirit: Drawing on the Power of Art to Tap the Magic & Wisdom Within*. New York: HarperCollins Publishers, 1992

Douglas, Scott. *Strange Angels and Other Plays*. Kelowna: Wood Lake Books, 2004

Erlander, Dan. *Manna and Mercy: A Brief History of God's Unfolding Promise to Mend the Entire Universe*. Mercer Island: The Order of Saints Martin and Teresa, 1992

Fox, Matthew. *Creativity: Where the Divine and the Human Meet*. New York: Jeremy P. Tarcher/Penguin, 2002

Hall, Sarah. *The Color of Light: Commissioning Stained Glass for a Church*. Chicago: Liturgy Training Publications, 1999

Hall, Sarah, and Bob Shantz. *Windows on Our Souls: A Spiritual Excavation*. Ottawa: Novalis, 2007

Huey-Heck, Lois, and Jim Kalnin. *The Spirituality of Art*. Kelowna: Northstone, 2006

Impastato, David. *Upholding Mystery: An Anthology of Contemporary Christian Poetry*. New York: Oxford University Press, 1997

Kapikian, Catherine. *Art in Service of the Sacred*. Nashville: Abingdon Press, 2006

Krondorfer, Björn, ed. *Body and Bible: Interpreting and Experiencing Biblical Narratives*. Philadelphia: Trinity Press International, 1992

L'Engle, Madeleine. *Walking on Water: Reflections on Faith & Art*. Wheaton: Harold Shaw Publishers, 1980

Lipsey, Roger. *Angelic Mistakes: The Art of Thomas Merton*. Boston & London: New Seeds, 2006

MacFarlane, Mary Anne and E. Ann Fleming, eds. *Arts and the Spirit: The Role of Art in Faith Formation*. Toronto: United Church Publishing House, 2007

McCollough, Charles. *The Art of Parables: Reinterpreting the Teaching Stories of Jesus in Word & Scripture*. Kelowna: CopperHouse, 2008

Nachmanovitch, Stephen. *Free Play: Improvisation in Life and Art*. New York: Jeremy P. Tarcher/Putnam, 1990

Nouwen, Henri. *Behold the Beauty of the Lord: Praying with Icons*. Notre Dame: Ave Maria Press, 1987

Porter, Phil with Cynthia Winton-Henry. *Having It All: Body, Mind, Heart & Spirit Together Again At Last*. Oakland: Wing It! Press, 1997

Ryan, Thomas. Soul Fire: *Accessing Your Creativity*. Woodstock: Skylight Paths Publishing, 2008

Saliers, Don and Emily Saliers. *A Song to Sing, A Life to Live: Reflections on Music as Spiritual Practice*. San Francisco: Jossey-Bass, 2005

Snowber, Celeste. *Embodied Prayer: Towards Wholeness of Body Mind Soul*. Kelowna: Northstone, 2004

Sojourners, ed. *Spirit of Fire: Faith, Art, and Action*. Washington, DC: Sojourners, 2003

Vrudny, Kimberly, and Wilson Yates, eds. *Arts, Theology, and the Church: New Intersections*. Cleveland: Pilgrim Press, 2005

Winton-Henry, Cynthia with Phil Porter. *What the Body Wants*. Kelowna: Northstone, 2004

Wolfe, Gregory. *Intruding upon the Timeless: Meditations on Art, Faith, and Mystery*. Baltimore: Square Halo Books, 2003

Wotton, Sally Armour. *Staging the Story: New Plays for Worship and Church Gatherings*. Toronto: United Church Publishing House, 1998

Wuthnow, Robert. *All In Sync: How Music and Art Are Revitalizing American Religion*. Berkeley and Los Angeles: University of California Press, 2003

Wuthnow, Robert. *Creative Spirituality: The Way of the Artist*. Berkeley and Los Angeles: University of California Press, 2001

Periodicals

ARTS: The Arts in Religious and Theological Studies, United Theological Seminary of the Twin Cities, 3000 Fifth Street Northwest, New Brighton, MN 55112; www.artsmag.org

Image: A Journal of the Arts and Religion, 3307 Third Ave. West, Seattle, WA 98119; www.imagejournal.org

Sacred Dance Guild Journal, Sacred Dance Guild, 550M Ritchie Highway, #271, Severna Park, MD 21146; www.sacreddanceguild.org

SEEN, Christians in the Visual Arts, 255 Grapevine Road, Wenham, MA 01984-1813; www.civa.org

Weavings: A Journal of Christian Spiritual Life (See especially March/April 2002 "Creativity") Upper Room Ministries, 1908 Grand Avenue, P.O. Box 340004, Nashville, TN 37203-0004; www.upperroom.org/weavings

Permissions

Beauty: Touching the Divine
Chapter 14, (pp. 201–14) from *Christianity for the Rest of Us: How the Neighborhood Church Is Transforming the Faith* by Diana Butler Bass. Copyright © 2006 by Diana Butler Bass. Reprinted by permission of HarperCollins Publishers.

The House of Love
Excerpted from *Behold the Beauty of the Lord*, by Henri J. M. Nouwen. Copyright © 1987 by Ave Maria Press, P.O. Box 428, Notre Dame, Indiana, 46556, www.avemariapress.com. Used with permission of the publisher.

Picture Summary: Rublev, Andrei (1360–c.1430); Icon of the Old Testament Trinity, c. 1410; Tretyakov Gallery, Moscow, Russia; Photo credit Scala/Art Resource, NY.

Cooperative Endeavor with the Spirit
Reprinted from the July-August 1996 edition of *Compass* (Vol. 14, #3). Used by permission.

Taking Flight
Art and photo © Melissa Richeson-O'Neil.

Tuning the E String
Copyright © 2002 by The Christian Century. Reprinted by permission from the November 20–December 3, 2002, issue of *The Christian Century*.

Revealing New Signs
Drawing by Thomas Merton. Used with permission of the Merton Legacy Trust and the Thomas Merton Center at Bellarmine University.

Into the Heart of the Other: Interfaith Story Circles
Reprinted from *God's Friends* (Volume 15, Number 1) © 2004 All Saints Company. Used by permission.

Creativity-Inspiring Titles from Wood Lake Publishing
www.woodlakebooks.com

The Spirituality of Art

Lois Huey-Heck and Jim Kalnin

This book is stunning with its beautiful full colour
reproductions of art across time, place and culture.

ISBN 978-1-896836-78-2

The Art of Parables

Reinterpreting the Teaching Stories of Jesus in Word & Form

Charles McCollough

Explores the parables of Jesus in a unique way that
honours the contribution of the arts

ISBN 978-1-55145-563-1

The Emerging Church

A Model for Change & a Map for Renewal

Bruce Sanguin

Want to move the culture of your congregation towards a pro-
gressive form of Christianity? Unsure how to make this shift?
Bruce Sanguin shares real-life examples from his own church
to help ministers and congregations as they move towards the
emerging vision of Christianity.

ISBN 978-1-55145-566-2

Writing The Sacred

A Psalm-inspired Path to Appreciating and
Writing Sacred Poetry

Ray McGinnis

Create poetry and prose from your heart. Full of practical
insights.

ISBN 978-1-896836-73-7

A Voluptuous God

A Christian Heretic Speaks

Robert V. Thompson

While "voluptuous" may not be a word most of us associate with "God", Bob Thompson speaks metaphorically of God being delicious, of God taking pleasure in simple things, of God knowing "that laughter is the best medicine, that only love can heal what ails us and only joy can cause our hearts to sing". Thompson calls us to worship a God of intimacy rather than a God of distance.

ISBN 978-1-55145-558-7

What the Body Wants

From InterPlay

Cynthia Winton-Henry with Phil Porter

Introduces readers into InterPlay, a practice for creative and spiritual development that reintegrates the body into all aspects of life. Includes audio CD.

ISBN 978-1-896836-66-9

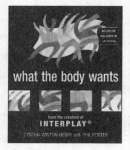

The Spirituality of Mazes & Labyrinths

Gailand MacQueen

Uses myth, history, and personal experience to explore the meanings of mazes and labyrinths. Illustrated in colour.

ISBN 978-1-896836-69-0

The Spirituality of Music

John Bird

Journey into the heart and soul of the music that forms the soundtrack of our lives. Filled with beautiful art and photographs.

ISBN 978-1-896836-88-1

Embodied Prayer
Towards Wholeness of Body, Mind, Soul
Celeste Snowber
An invitation to experience prayer from the inside out, awakening our soul through our bodies, allowing us to integrate our body, mind, and soul.
ISBN 978-1-896836-62-1

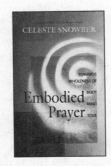

Finding The Still Point
A Spirituality of Balance
Tom Harpur
Focuses on using a spiritual approach to coping with stress and anxiety.
ISBN 978-1-896836-71-3

Darwin, Divinity, and the Dance of the Cosmos
An Ecological Christianity
Bruce Sanguin
For those ready and willing to embark on an exciting theological journey of discovery, this book represents a rich opportunity to become reacquainted with the Spirit of God moving in and through the very dynamics of an unfolding universe.
ISBN 978-1-55145-545-7

Experiencing the Heart Of Christianity
Tim Scorer
A 12-session program for groups based on Marcus Borg's bestseller. Incluces DVD.
ISBN 978-1-55145-511-2

Living The Heart of Christianity

A Guide to Putting Your Faith into Action

Marcus Borg and Tim Scorer

A companion to Borg's bestseller that helps individuals put their faith into action.

ISBN 978-1-55145-543-3

Songs for the Holy One

Psalms and Refrains for Worship

Thomas Barnett and Donald Patriquin

Using inclusive language and paired with original refrains, the 150 Psalms have been translated into engaging and reverent renditions.

Hidden Coil Bind

ISBN 978-1-55145-497-9

More Voices

225 songs – theologicaly balanced, refreshing, inspirational, contempory, and global music.

ISBN 978-1-55134-148-4

Wood Lake Publishing also distributes the music of Linnea Good, Jim and Jean Strathdee, and Bruce & Cheryl Harding and many others. Visit our website: www.woodlakebooks.com